The Dorling Kindersley

ILLUSTRATED
FAMILY
ENCYCLOPEDIA

VOLUME 6 CONTENTS, EUROPE, CENTRAL – GARDENS

LONDON, NEW YORK, MUNICH,
MELBOURNE AND DELHI

Senior Editor Jayne Parsons   **Senior Art Editor** Gillian Shaw

Project Editors
Marian Broderick, Gill Cooling,
Maggie Crowley, Hazel Egerton,
Cynthia O'Neill, Veronica Pennycook,
Louise Pritchard, Steve Setford, Jackie Wilson

Project Art Editors
Jane Felstead, Martyn Foote,
Neville Graham, Jamie Hanson,
Christopher Howson, Jill Plank, Floyd Sayers,
Jane Tetzlaff, Ann Thompson

Editors
Rachel Beaugié, Nic Kynaston, Sarah Levete,
Karen O'Brien, Linda Sonntag

Art Editors
Tina Borg, Diane Clouting,
Tory Gordon-Harris

DTP Designers
Andrew O'Brien, Cordelia Springer

Managing Editor Ann Kramer   **Managing Art Editor** Peter Bailey

Senior DTP Designer Mathew Birch

Picture Research Jo Walton, Kate Duncan, Liz Moore

DK Picture Library Ola Rudowska, Melanie Simmonds

Country pages by PAGE*One*: Bob Gordon, Helen Parker,
Thomas Keenes, Sarah Watson, Chris Clark

Cartographers Peter Winfield, James Anderson

Research Robert Graham, Angela Koo

Editorial Assistants Sarah-Louise Reed, Nichola Roberts

Production Louise Barratt, Charlotte Traill

First published in Great Britain in 1997, 2004
by Dorling Kindersley Limited,
80 Strand, London WC2R 0RL

This edition published in 2004 by MDS BOOKS/MEDIASAT Group in association with MediaFund Limited

www.mediasatgroup.com

A CIP catalogue record for this book is available from the British Library

ISBN: 84 9789 537 1 (ISBN of the collection)
ISBN: 84 9789 526 6 (ISBN of this volume)
ISSN: 1744 2214

Not to be sold separately from the Daily Mail

Colour reproduction by Colourscan, Singapore
Printed and bound in the E.U.

EUROPE, CENTRAL (CONT.)

Poland

This country of medieval towns and scattered villages has a history of invasion and occupation by foreign powers. From 1945 to 1989, Poland was a communist state. Since the collapse of communism, however, Poland has been experiencing massive economic, social, and political change. It joined the EU in 2004.

Warsaw

Poland's capital since the 1500s, Warsaw was almost completely destroyed during World War II (1939–45). Working from original plans, paintings, and photographs, the Poles have rebuilt the city, restoring its ancient landmarks and treasured buildings. Today, the reconstructed buildings line wide streets and squares.

Old Town Square

Beet

Potato

Sugar beet

Root crops

Poland is a major producer of rye, and also of root crops such as potatoes, sugar beets, and beets. Nearly half the land is used to grow crops or raise livestock, particularly pigs. State farms account for about 10 per cent of this land. Most privately owned farms are small, producing some crops to sell, and the rest to feed farmers' families. Farming employs a quarter of Poland's work-force.

Wheat

Poland's leading grain crop is wheat, although yields are poor. Two-thirds of the wheat is fed to livestock, some, with potatoes, is used to distil vodka, and with the rest, farmers bake bread.

People

Like the neighbouring Czechs and Slovaks, Poles originate from the Slavic peoples of Europe. Poland has few ethnic minorities, and more than 95 per cent of the people are Polish-speaking Roman Catholics. Many Poles have a traditional way of life; local folk arts and crafts flourish. These include wood carving and colourful embroidery.

POLAND FACTS

CAPITAL CITY	Warsaw
AREA	312,685 sq km (120,728 sq miles)
POPULATION	38,600,000
DENSITY	127 per sq km (328 per sq mile)
MAIN LANGUAGE	Polish
MAJOR RELIGION	Christian
CURRENCY	Zloty
LIFE EXPECTANCY	73 years
PEOPLE PER DOCTOR	435
GOVERNMENT	Multiparty democracy
ADULT LITERACY	99%

Industry

About one-fifth of Poland's labour force works in industry, but production in the huge old Soviet-style factories is inefficient. In order to compete on the free market, the government is slowly privatizing industry. Shipbuilding is an important industry on the Baltic Coast, and the Gdansk shipyard is one of several. Poland has a thriving iron and steel industry, and big reserves of coal, lignite (brown coal), copper, lead, silver, and zinc.

Czech Republic

The Czech Republic consists of the two ancient states of Bohemia and Moravia, which once formed part of the Holy Roman Empire. From 1918, it was part of Czechoslovakia and only emerged as an independent country in 1993, when Czechoslovakia was partitioned. The Czech Republic is central Europe's most industrialized nation, and manufacturing employs 40 per cent of its work-force.

Prague

One of the most beautiful capital cities in Europe, Prague has remained virtually unchanged for centuries. Today, it plays host to an increasing number of visitors who come for both business and pleasure. However, air pollution caused by nearby factories poses a major problem.

St. Nicholas's Church

Farming

Only five per cent of the Czech work-force is employed in farming. Much of the land is controlled by large farms owned by the state or cooperatives. Czech farms have some of the highest grain yields in central Europe, but most is fed to livestock because the Republic specializes in meat and milk production.

Bohemian glass

Since the 1300s, the Bohemians of the south have made beautifully decorated glass from the fine sands found in this region. Bohemian glass is prized for its high quality, elegance, and delicacy.

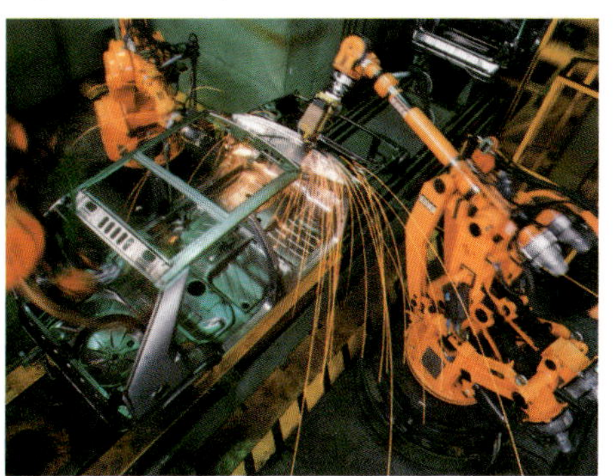

CZECH REPUBLIC FACTS

CAPITAL CITY	Prague
AREA	78,866 sq km (30,450 sq miles)
POPULATION	10,300,000
DENSITY	131 per sq km (388 per sq mile)
MAIN LANGUAGE	Czech
MAJOR RELIGION	Christian
CURRENCY	Czech koruna
LIFE EXPECTANCY	75 years
PEOPLE PER DOCTOR	333
GOVERNMENT	Multiparty democracy
ADULT LITERACY	99%

Beer

Czech beers are popular all over the world, and Budweiser, Budvar, and Pilsner are household names. Brewing traditions go back hundreds of years.

Industry

The break-up of the communist regime led to the privatization of many Czech companies. However, some of the very large factories, such as the Skoda works at Plzen, remain under state control. Czech factories are able to produce about 200,000 cars a year. As well as cars, Skoda produces locomotives, machine tools, and weapons. The Czechs also produce iron and steel, machinery, and transport equipment, although there is a trend to move away from heavy industry into consumer goods such as textiles.

E

Slovakia

Slovakia was the rural and poorer half of Czechoslovakia, and after its independence in 1993, the country suffered economically. Much of the land is mountainous and forested. About half is used for crops or grazing, but industry now employs a large number of workers. Most people are Slovaks, speaking their own language, but there are also some Roma and Czechs, as well as a nine per cent Hungarian minority.

SLOVAKIA FACTS

CAPITAL CITY	Bratislava
AREA	48,845 sq km (18,859 sq miles)
POPULATION	5,400,000
MAIN LANGUAGE	Slovak
MAJOR RELIGION	Christian
CURRENCY	Slovak Koruna

Bratislava

From 1536 to 1784, Bratislava was the capital of Hungary. Now it is the capital of an independent Slovakia. The city was founded in the 10th century, and has had a university since 1467. The new parliament buildings were once the home of an archbishop. Bratislava is a Danube river port and a rail centre. Its factories make chemicals and engineering goods.

Rural life

The Slovakian countryside is a mixture of mountain villages, ancient walled towns, and castles. There are still many large state-run farms, but about 20 per cent of the land is farmed by tiny, family-run concerns. The main crops are potatoes, sugar beet, and grains. Rural life is hard, and poverty is common, driving increasing numbers of young people to towns in search of work.

Folklore

Folk traditions are strong in Slovakia, where puppet shows are popular. The former Czechoslovakia is acknowledged as the original home of European puppetry. The Slovakian people enjoy folk festivals where they can dress in regional costumes and sing and dance to traditional music.

Wooden puppet

Hungary

Hungary was formed about a thousand years ago by the Magyars, an ethnic group from Russia that makes up 90 per cent of today's population. Hungary was communist from 1945 until 1990, and since then its industries have had to compete on the world market. The country's skilled scientists and engineers have succeeded in attracting foreign investment.

Thermal springs

Hungary has hundreds of hot thermal springs; their warm mineral waters are said to have medicinal properties. The country has more than 150 spring baths, which are open to the public.

HUNGARY FACTS

CAPITAL CITY	Budapest
AREA	93,030 sq km (35,919 sq miles)
POPULATION	9,900,000
DENSITY	107 per sq km (278 per sq mile)
MAIN LANGUAGE	Hungarian (Magyar)
MAJOR RELIGION	Christian
CURRENCY	Forint
LIFE EXPECTANCY	71 years
PEOPLE PER DOCTOR	313
GOVERNMENT	Multiparty democracy
ADULT LITERACY	99%

Goulash is a traditional Hungarian stew.

Wine

Hungary is a world-class wine producer and exports a wide range of high-quality red and white wines. The best known Hungarian wine is Tokay, pronounced tok-eye. It is a sweet, rich, golden wine, widely believed to be healthful. Another well-known Hungarian wine is Bull's Blood, so-called for its dark blood-red colour.

Paprika

Hungarians grow more than 40 per cent of the world's paprika, a sweet, bright-red pepper used in cooking. One town, Kalocsa in southern Hungary, even has a museum devoted entirely to this spice. Paprika originally came from Central America. Hungarian farmers also grow rye, corn, wheat, barley, sugar beets, and potatoes, as well as grapes, olives, and figs. Sunflowers are grown for their oil.

Goulash

Hungary's most famous dish is goulash, a stew of beef with vegetables, flavoured and coloured with paprika. A pork version is called *pörkhölt*. Other traditional dishes with paprika include bacon and potato casserole, and chicken paprikash.

Budapest

Straddling the Danube, Budapest is two cities in one – Buda on the hilly right bank, and Pest on the low-lying left bank. Buda was the old royal capital of Hungary, and has fine old buildings and the remains of a Roman town. Pest is the country's administrative and industrial centre.

The Parliament buildings in Pest, viewed from Buda

Horse breeding

Hungary has a long tradition of horse breeding, located at the great stud farms at Mezöhegyes and Bábolna. The best-known Hungarian breeds are the Nonius and Furioso, which were developed at Mezöhegyes, and the Shagya Arab at Bábolna. Today, these stud farms develop horses for taking part in shows.

Hungary's oldest stud farm at Mezöhegyes

 FIND OUT MORE   CHRISTIANITY   EMPIRES   EUROPE   EUROPE, HISTORY OF   FARMING   GOVERNMENTS AND POLITICS   HOLY ROMAN EMPIRE   HORSES   SOVIET UNION

EUROPEAN UNION

TWENTY-FIVE COUNTRIES have joined together to form the European Union (EU). But Europe was not always united. Between 1870 and 1945, France and Germany were at war three times. Determined to ensure that their two countries never fought again, the French and Germans decided to link their coal and steel industries so that their nations would be forced to work together. The creation of the European Coal and Steel Community (ECSC) in 1951 led to today's European Union.

The euro

On 1 January 2002, a single currency, the euro, was fully launched in 12 countries of the European Union (EU). The notes and coins of this new currency replaced the national currencies of those nations. The only EU countries to stay out of the monetary union were Britain, Denmark, and Sweden.

Uniting Europe

In 1957, the ECSC evolved into the wider European Economic Community (EEC). Ten years later this became the European Community (EC). In 1991, EC leaders signed the Maastricht Treaty, which started Europe towards full economic and monetary union. When the treaty came into force in 1993, the EC became the European Union (EU).

The growing union

The European Union has 25 members. A number of states have applied for membership, with more considering joining. Trade and cooperation agreements are already in place between the EU and many applicants. Switzerland has close trade links with the EU, but a national referendum in 2001 rejected joining.

Date of joining: 1957, 1973, 1981, 1986, 1995, 2004

Members of the EU, 2004

Structure of the EU

The EU has three main institutions: the Commission, based in Brussels, Belgium, is the civil service which runs the EU; the Parliament, in Strasbourg, France, and Brussels, provides control over the EU; the European Court of Justice, in Luxembourg, makes sure EU laws are applied properly.

European Parliament

Every five years, adults throughout the EU go to the polls to elect 732 Members of the European Parliament (MEPs) to represent their interests. Although it does not have the same powers as a national parliament, the European Parliament advises the Commission and supervises its work and annual budget.

What the EU does

The European Union has many different roles covering economic, financial, commercial, political, industrial, agricultural, social, and cultural matters. Its two main achievements have been to establish free trade between the member states by abolishing customs duties, and to set up a common agricultural and fisheries policy.

EU aid

The EU provides subsidies to the less well-off regions of Europe, for projects such as developing new industries. Much EU aid is targeted towards improving transport links in Europe, such as building roads and railways, so all regions can share in the benefits of the single market.

Jean Monnet

Jean Monnet (1888–1979) was a French economist who convinced the French foreign minister, Robert Schuman (1886–1963), that the only way to avoid another war between France and Germany was to integrate their coal and steel industries. The ECSC was set up with Monnet as its first president. His vision led directly to the development of today's EU.

Agricultural policy

In order to guarantee food supplies and increase agricultural productivity, the EU runs a very complex Common Agricultural Policy (CAP). This has established free movement of farm produce throughout the EU.

The EU has sponsored a common European passport.

Social policy

The EU tries to improve employment for unemployed workers and young people by investing in education and training in deprived regions. It has also established a common Social Chapter of Workers' Rights.

Timeline

1951 European Coal and Steel Community (ECSC) is set up.

1957 The ECSC nations sign the Treaty of Rome, setting up the European Economic Community (EEC);

1967 ECSC, EEC, and Euratom merge to form the European Community (EC).

1979 European Monetary System set up to link currencies.

1991 Maastricht Treaty sets out timetable for full economic union.

1993 EC becomes the European Union (EU).

2002 The euro replaces existing currencies in 12 EU countries.

2004 Ten additional countries become members of the EU.

FIND OUT MORE — EUROPE, HISTORY OF · FARMING · FISHING INDUSTRY · FOOD · MONEY · TRADE AND INDUSTRY · WORLD WAR II

EUROPEAN WILDLIFE

EUROPE IS A landmass that contains many different habitats, ranging from the Arctic tundra, through broad-leaved forests, and mountainous areas, to dry, hot regions around the Mediterranean. Only deserts and tropical forests are missing from the list. European wildlife is not as rich as it once was; human intervention in the form of agriculture and forest clearance, as well as the sheer size of the human population, has diminished the number of plants and animals. Yet in undisturbed forests and wetlands, a large diversity of wildlife remains.

Broad-leaved woodland wildlife

Broad-leaved woodlands extend across Europe. The trees within them, such as oaks and sycamores, are broad-leaved, or deciduous, trees, which means they lose their leaves in winter. In spring and summer, when the leaves reappear and plants bloom, woodlands support many insects, birds, and mammals, such as squirrels and mice.

Oak tree
Commonly found in broad-leaved woodlands, oaks provide homes and food for many animals. Insects, for example, feed on leaves and other parts of the tree, while they themselves are food for larger animals, such as birds. Acorns, the fruits of the oak, appear in late summer.

Dappled coats help to camouflage deer as they graze on grass.

Once acorns have fallen to the ground, they provide a nutritious meal for birds, squirrels, and mice.

Female nut weevil drilling into acorn with her mouthparts.

Rostrum

Red fox
Red foxes live on their own or in small family groups in underground dens. They are most active at night when they hunt for rabbits, rodents, and worms. They may also eat fish and fruit.

Females flick their large, bushy tails to warn cubs of danger.

Fallow deer
Woodland provides cover and food for fallow deer. Females and young live in small herds. Males have antlers, and are solitary or live in small groups. Males and females meet during the mating season in the autumn.

Nut weevil
This beetle lives on oak trees, feeding on buds and leaves. It has a snout-like rostrum, at the end of which are its jaws. In late summer, the female makes holes in the oak's acorns. In each hole she deposits an egg. The larva that hatches from the egg feeds on the acorn.

Wetland wildlife

Europe's wetlands are rich in wildlife. Reeds, bulrushes, and marsh plants provide food and shelter for wetland animals, such as voles and otters. Insects and other invertebrates are a food source for fish and frogs, which themselves are eaten by many water birds.

Bulrushes provide nesting sites for birds.

Flower head

Bulrushes
These tall grass-like plants grow at the fringes of lakes and ponds. Their roots are often in wet soil or submerged in water, while their stems and leaves extend above the water. Bulrushes have dark, compact, cylindrical flower heads.

European kingfisher
This small bird hunts for fish and other water animals from a perch along the banks of streams and lakes. Once prey is spotted, the kingfisher plunges into the water, grabs it with its long, pointed beak, and returns to the perch to eat its meal.

European otter
Otters are strong swimmers, adapted for rapid movement in water. An otter's body is long and streamlined, its dense, glossy fur is water-repellent, and it has webbed feet. Otters hunt underwater, catching prey such as fish, water birds, and frogs. They are equally agile on land, and catch water voles and other animals that live on riverbanks.

Water vole
Water voles are good swimmers. They build tunnels in banks next to lakes and slow-moving rivers. These tunnels have chambers for food storage and nesting, and entrances that open above and below the waterline.

Edible frog
Edible frogs live in marshes and lakes, sometimes emerging at night to feed on land. They catch insects with their long, sticky tongues. Larger prey, such as newts and small fish, are caught in the jaws and pushed into the mouth with the feet.

Water voles feed on plants, roots, and bulbs.

Alpine chough
In summer, choughs live in flocks above the tree line. They walk over rocky ground, probing under vegetation and in crevices for insects and snails. They glide on air currents, coping easily with the strong gusts of wind found at high altitude.

Mountain wildlife

The Alps and the Pyrenees are the major mountains of Europe. Vegetation changes with increasing altitude; each zone has its characteristic wildlife. Animals tend to move to lower altitudes during the cold winter months when food becomes scarce.

Mouflon
The mouflon is a wild sheep that lives in remote, mountainous regions. It feeds on grasses and other plants during the day, and rests at night. The mouflon is surefooted, moving easily over rough terrain. Males bang their heads and horns together when competing for mates.

Alpine meadow
Alpine meadows are found above the tree line and below the snow line. In summer, they are covered in a blanket of bright flowers and dwarf shrubs. These provide food for hordes of insects, which in turn are eaten by birds. Meadow vegetation is also eaten by grazing animals.

Bears eat rodents, deer, insects, salmon, carrion, tubers, and berries.

Cubs are born in dens in mid-winter.

Brown bear
These large bears live in remote forested areas of mountains and as far north as the tundra. They have no natural enemies apart from humans. In winter, brown bears usually retire to a den for a period of dormancy.

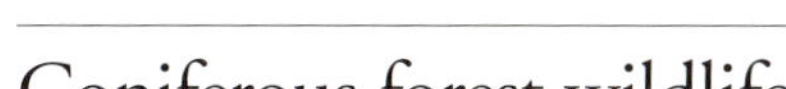

Coniferous forest wildlife

Coniferous forests of evergreen trees, such as spruce and pine, extend across northern Europe. They are dense and dark, with few ground plants. Summers are warm; winters are cold, with heavy snow falls. Many animals eat the leaves and seeds of conifers.

Norway spruce
Norway spruces have reddish trunks, dark green crowns, and grow up to 55 m (180 ft) in height. These seeds of the spruce, as well as the bark, buds, and needle-like leaves, provide food for forest animals.

Triangular outline prevents snow accumulating and snapping branches.

Pine marten
Pine martens hunt in the morning and evening, using their excellent hearing and sight to locate birds, squirrels, rabbits, and rats.

Pine martens climb trees, resting by day in tree hollows.

Common crossbill
The common or red crossbill lives in the forest canopy and is rarely seen on the ground, except when it lands to drink. Its crossed beak provides the bird with a strong "tool" for prising open the scales of pine and spruce cones. It then uses its tongue to extract the seeds.

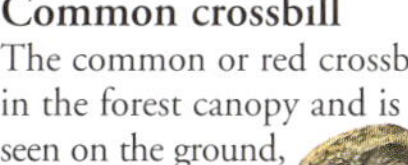

Upper and lower parts of bill are crossed.

Arctic hare
The arctic hare lives in the coniferous forests and tundra of the far North. Its fur turns from brown in summer to white in winter, to conceal it from predators such as foxes.

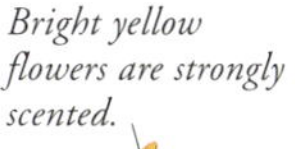

Bright yellow flowers are strongly scented.

Mediterranean wildlife

The Mediterranean region of Europe has hot, dry summers, and milder and wetter winters. Aromatic plants, such as thyme, and trees such as cedar grow here. Many animals survive by sheltering in midday heat; others migrate.

Black, bristly feathers give it its other name of bearded vulture.

Lammergeier
The lammergeier lives in mountainous areas. It eats carrion, including the bones, which it drops on to rocks from a height to smash them and expose the soft marrow.

Short antenna

Spanish festoon butterfly
This brightly patterned butterfly is found on the coasts of Spain, France, and Portugal. It can be seen from late winter, when temperatures start to rise, until early summer, when mating is complete.

Zig-zag wing pattern

Ear tufts are used to signal to other lynxes.

Common lizard
A common sight in southern Europe during the summer, this lizard sunbathes in the morning to increase its body temperature, making it more active when searching for insects.

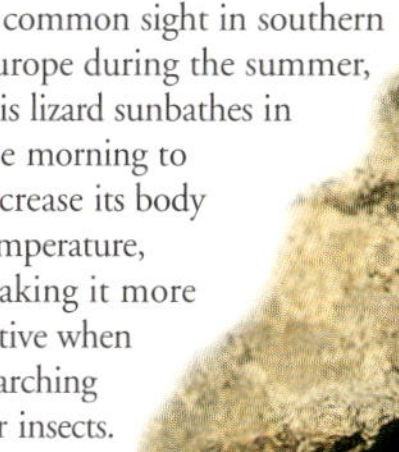

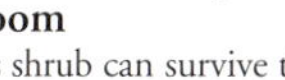

Broom
This shrub can survive the hot, dry conditions of the Mediterranean summer. The seed pods produced by the flowers dry in the sun, and split open to scatter the tiny seeds.

Spanish lynx
This cat, once found all over Spain, is now restricted to the pine forests, scrub, and sand dunes of the Coto Doñana National Park in southwest Spain. Lynx feed on rabbits and hares, deer fawns, and ducks.

FIND OUT MORE   BIRDS OF PREY   FORESTS   LAKE AND RIVER WILDLIFE   MARSH AND SWAMP WILDLIFE

EVOLUTION

THE TERM EVOLUTION refers to the theory that existing animals and plants have evolved, or developed, through a process of continual change from previous life forms. Some scientists argue that by looking at fossil evidence we can find out more about the past. Fossils have shown that primitive life forms appeared more than 3.8 billion years ago, and that vertebrates existed at least 500 million years ago. Over generations, better-adapted organisms have developed.

How a species evolves

An organism may undergo change due to a number of processes, such as natural selection and adaptation, induced by the environment in which it lives. For example, selection may have promoted larger and faster horses adapted for living on open grassy plains. In some cases, a subspecies can change so much that it becomes very different from the rest of its species.

Hyracotherium, the first in a long line of horses, appeared approximately 55 million years ago.

Four-toed hoof

Equus (modern horse) evolved around 1.64 million years ago. It originated as a plains grazer, and has a single toe forming a hoof.

One-toed hoof

Long limbs developed for speed.

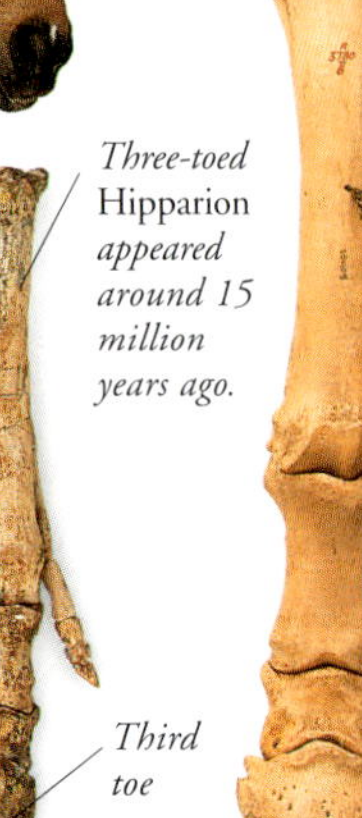

The third toe became larger until the side toes eventually disappeared.

Three-toed Hipparion appeared around 15 million years ago.

Third toe

Foot of early four-toed *Hyracotherium*

Foot of three-toed *Hipparion*

Hoof of modern horse, *Equus*

Natural selection

The theory of natural selection suggests that environmental factors may favour some members of a species over others, enabling the fittest to survive. Experiments with the carnivorous plant, sundew, backed this theory. Plants that were fed meat produced more flowers and seeds than plants which were not.

Plant fed meat produces flowers.

Unfed plant has fewer flowers.

Heredity

Heredity studies how characteristics of certain individuals are passed on from one generation to the next. This process often involves the expression of a parent's dominant gene, which may mask the effect of the recessive gene.

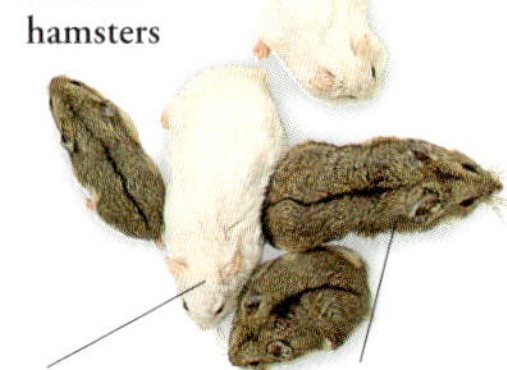

Russian hamsters

Recessive albino gene

Dominant grey gene

Variation

Variation refers to the differences within a species. Certain variations, such as shell colour, may give certain individuals advantages over others. These individuals will have a greater chance of surviving and reproducing.

Banded snails

Shell colours allow snail to adapt to local habitat.

Mutations

Occasionally during reproduction, the process of replicating genetic material (DNA) goes wrong and produces an accidental mutation. Normally, these mutants do not live but some survive as an important source of variation on which selection operates.

Fuller's mutant teasel has curved spines, allowing easier seed dispersal.

Teasel plant

Sexual selection

Some animals choose their mates by means of sexual selection. A male, may have elaborate features, such as bright feathers, to attract a mate. Characteristics such as these, which may be beneficial to the species, are passed to the next generation.

Peacock

Adaptation

The process of adaptation occurs when an organism evolves in a certain way to make it better suited to its environment. Some people believe that this can lead to a new species, and that an animal or a plant will adapt to its surroundings so that it has a better chance of survival.

Darwin's finches

While visiting the Galápagos Islands, English naturalist Charles Darwin (1809–82) noticed the variety of finches living there. Because they resembled finches of mainland South America, he argued that each finch species had evolved a differently shaped beak to meet the needs of its particular diet.

Plant-feeding finch

Insect-feeding finch

Monarch butterfly

Viceroy butterfly

Mimicry in butterflies

Mimicry is a form of adaptation where one species has developed a resemblance to another as a means of protection. Birds find the monarch butterfly distasteful, but also avoid the similarly coloured viceroy, even though it is palatable.

Intermediates

Intermediates are thought to be the "halfway" species that should exist if one group of organism has evolved from another. In 1861, discovery of the earliest fossil bird, *Archaeopteryx*, provided important support for this theory. The fossil clearly combines the reptile characteristics of a dinosaur in its skeleton, but at the same time has the uniquely bird-like feature of feathers.

Lungfish

Living intermediates

The lungfish can breathe oxygen directly from air and has paired fleshy fins for swimming. Lungfish arose about 380 million years ago when animals first stepped on land; it is thought that the first land-going tetrapods (four-footed animals) evolved from lungfish-like intermediates.

Human impact

For centuries humans have had an impact on animal and plant habitats. For example, some animals have had to adapt to new environments created by human settlement and industry. Also, by selective breeding, scientists have altered the genetic make-up of some plants and animals to create superior crops and meat for human consumption. Fruits, such as grapes and oranges, have been bred so that they no longer have seeds and are therefore easier to digest.

Tomatoes are bred to have a longer shelf life.

Seedless orange

Seedless grape

Artificial selection

Scientists can manipulate the genetic make-up of plants and animals by artificially selecting particular strains according to need. For instance, genetically altered products, such as tomatoes with enhanced flavour, are already on sale. Dog breeders, too, can alter the temperament, shape, size, and colour of dogs. The ability to alter genetic make-up raises many ethical questions.

Shar pei dog

Impact by pollution

It was discovered that during the Industrial Revolution, light coloured peppered moths, previously camouflaged from bird predators, became vulnerable on soot blackened trees. However, darker coloured peppered moths did survive and went on to breed more dark moths.

Peppered moths

Evidence

Much of the evidence for evolution is based on fossils. These show how life originated from simple forms in the sea and then evolved to occupy land, freshwater, and air. Study of the common characteristics of organisms suggest how they could be inter-related. Also, investigations into genetics and its molecular basis have led to a greater understanding of how evolution works.

Fossil evidence

Fossils of animals and plants show that there have been significant changes throughout geological time. Fossils show how the first land living plants appeared some 440 million years ago, but were not sufficiently well established to form forests until about 320 million years ago.

Fossil of fern plant

Molecular evidence

Often, if two new species evolve from a common ancestor, their DNA begins to change. For example, both the red and grey squirrel feed on acorns. However, the red squirrel lacks the digestive enzyme which breaks down chemicals in the acorn. This has led to a decline of red squirrels in the British Isles.

Grey squirrel population outnumbers that of the red squirrel in Britain

Creation theories

Evolutionists believe that life on Earth has evolved progressively over thousands of millions of years, originally from non-living materials. However, some people argue that all life forms on the Earth were created by design, in or close to the form in which they exist today. Although creationists as a group reject the theory of evolution, many accept that life forms on Earth can change. They believe that God created various kinds of creatures that have diversified within each kind until the present day.

19th-century caricature of Charles Darwin

The sturdy armadillo limb is adapted for digging.

Armadillo forelimb

Wrist bone

Finger digits

Upper arm

The chimpanzee's arm is very similar to the basic vertebrate bone pattern.

Chimpanzee's arm

In bats, the hand and finger bones developed into supports for the membranes of the wing.

Bones of bat's wing

Comparative anatomy

French naturalist Georges Cuvier (1769–1832) demonstrated that the function of the vertebrate skeleton reflects the way in which the animal lived. Since vertebrates have a common ancestry, the structure of the skeleton has a similar plan. Armadillo limb bones may be directly compared with the arm bones of a chimpanzee, and those of a bat's wing.

Jean Baptiste de Lamarck

French naturalist Jean Baptiste de Lamarck (1744–1829) proposed a theory of evolution that broke the prevailing idea of the fixity of species. He claimed that by striving to fit into their natural surroundings, organisms changed in bodily form, and that such transformations were passed on to their offspring. According to his theory the giraffe developed a long neck by stretching to eat leaves from trees.

EXPLORATION

SINCE THE EARLIEST TIMES, people have been curious about the world in which they live. For more than 3,000 years, explorers have charted most of Earth's surface by land and sea. Often these brave pioneers went out into the unknown inspired by more than mere curiosity. Sometimes they went in search of riches, or to find new and less overcrowded places to live, or in a quest for scientific knowledge. In the course of mapping the world, explorers quashed many myths while bringing back true stories that could seem even stranger than fiction.

Ancient exploration

In ancient times, peoples such as the Phoenicians explored new regions in their quest for trading partners. The Greeks and Romans also discovered more about the world as their empires expanded. People began to read about far-flung places in books by classical geographers such as Strabo (c.63 BC–c.AD 21).

Xuan Zang

The Buddhist monk Xuan Zang (602–664) was one of the greatest travellers of ancient China. In 629 he set off alone on the famed Silk Road to visit India, Nepal, Sri Lanka, and Pakistan, making friends for China and studying as he went. He returned in 654 laden with the finest Asian artworks. After Xuan Zang's death, the Emperor Gaodong built the Xingjiao monastery outside Xi'an to honour him.

Exploration for trade

After the Ottomans captured Constantinople in 1453, European rulers paid sailors to find alternatives to the land route to Asia. It was soon proved quicker and cheaper to ship luxury goods such as spices and silks by sea.

Han dynasty (206 BC–220 AD) figurine

Chinese jade horse

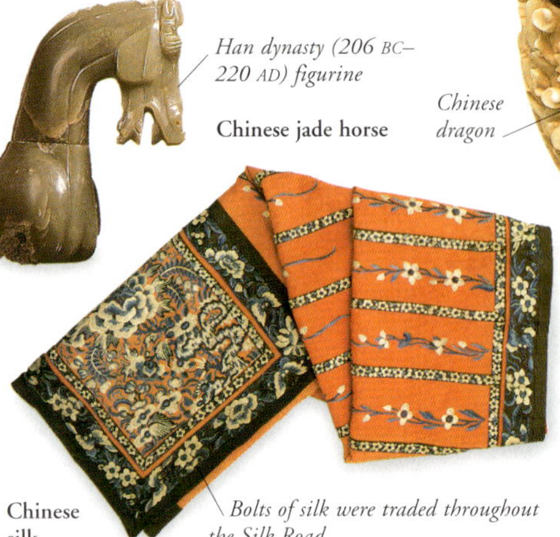

Chinese dragon

Ivory imperial seal

Chinese silk

Bolts of silk were traded throughout the Silk Road.

Silk Road

In ancient and medieval times, there was a 6,400-km (4,000-mile) overland trade route between China and Europe, known as the Silk Road. It fell into disuse when Asian and European traders adopted new east-to-west sea routes in the 15th and 16th centuries.

Marco Polo

The Venetian pioneer trader Marco Polo (c.1254–1324) travelled overland to China, and served the Emperor Kublai Khan as a diplomat for 17 years. Back in Europe, while in prison for debt (1296–98), he dictated a hugely popular book about life in the Far East. Centuries later it helped inspire Columbus to find a new westward sea route to the East.

Kublai Khan and Marco Polo

Mongol emperor Kublai Khan

Marco Polo

Clove tree

Spice Islands

Europeans knew that valuable spices, such as cloves, grew wild in the East, and some of the greatest explorations were efforts to find the Spice Islands, which are today known as the Moluccas. Portuguese, Spanish, Dutch, and British navigators all fought to control this valuable source of trade for their countries.

Vasco da Gama

Portuguese navigator Vasco da Gama (c.1469–1524) became the first European to sail to India when he landed at Calicut (Calcutta) in 1498. Da Gama returned twice: in 1502 to avenge the deaths of some Christian traders, and for the last time, in 1524, as Viceroy of India. He died shortly after this appointment.

Aztec sacrificial knife

New World

From 1492 Europeans aimed to reach India by sailing west. When they discovered that America was in their path, they hailed this continent as a "new world". But as they explored it, they brutally plundered and destroyed the rich empires of the Aztec, Inca, and Maya.

Aztec portrait beaker

Southern Continent

For centuries Europeans believed that there was a Terra Australis Incognita – or Unknown Southern Continent. In the 17th and 18th centuries Dutch and British seamen, such as James Cook (1728–79), began to explore it, and the great continent became known as Australia.

Robert O'Hara Burke and William J Wills

Early European settlement of Australia was coastal. Burke (1820–61) and Wills (1834–61) made the first journey from Melbourne across the continent's parched interior to the northern coast. On the way back, they died of starvation in the Outback.

Death at Cooper's Creek

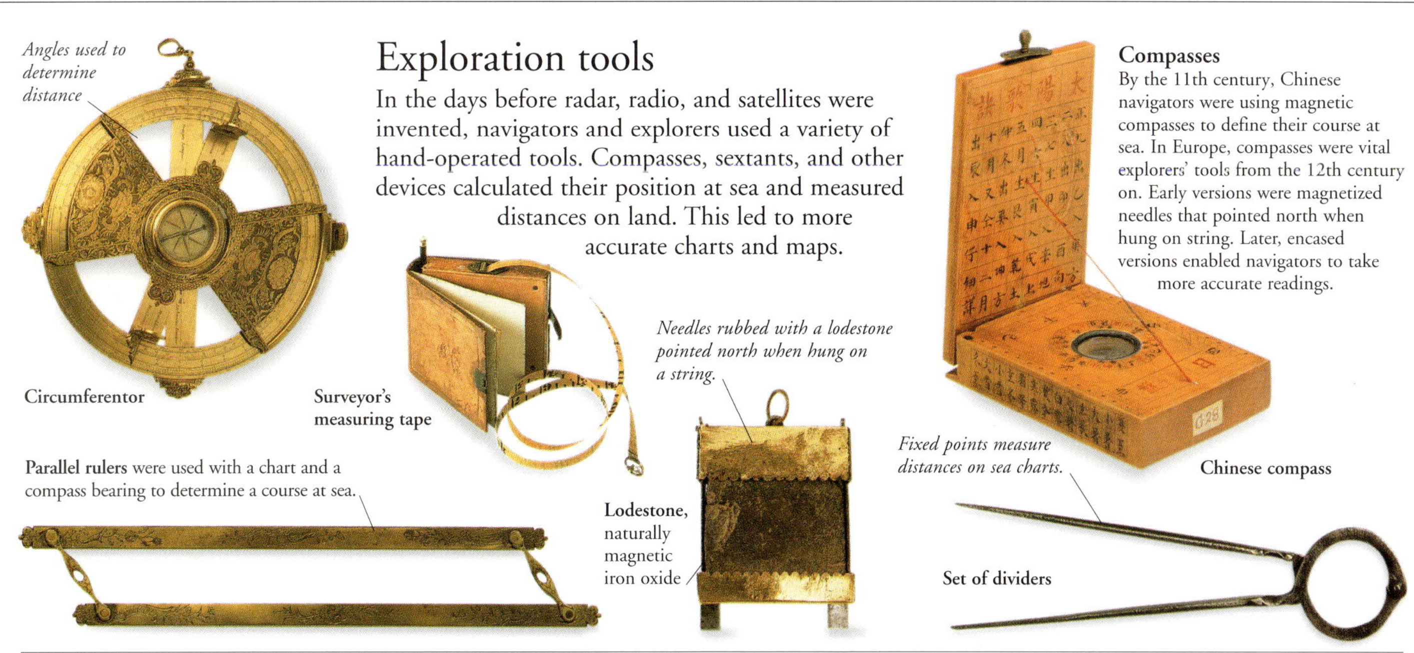

Exploration tools

In the days before radar, radio, and satellites were invented, navigators and explorers used a variety of hand-operated tools. Compasses, sextants, and other devices calculated their position at sea and measured distances on land. This led to more accurate charts and maps.

Angles used to determine distance

Circumferentor

Surveyor's measuring tape

Parallel rulers were used with a chart and a compass bearing to determine a course at sea.

Needles rubbed with a lodestone pointed north when hung on a string.

Lodestone, naturally magnetic iron oxide

Compasses

By the 11th century, Chinese navigators were using magnetic compasses to define their course at sea. In Europe, compasses were vital explorers' tools from the 12th century on. Early versions were magnetized needles that pointed north when hung on string. Later, encased versions enabled navigators to take more accurate readings.

Fixed points measure distances on sea charts.

Chinese compass

Set of dividers

Pundits

In the 19th century, the British in India trained Indian surveyors, known as pundits, to make maps of the Central Asian territories of Karakoram, the Hindu Kush, and the Himalaya. In 1863, one of the earliest pundits, Muhammad-i-Hameed, made the first recorded trip over the Karakoram range to Chinese Turkestan. He died after six months in Yarkand, but his surveying equipment and notebook containing vital topographical information were taken back to India.

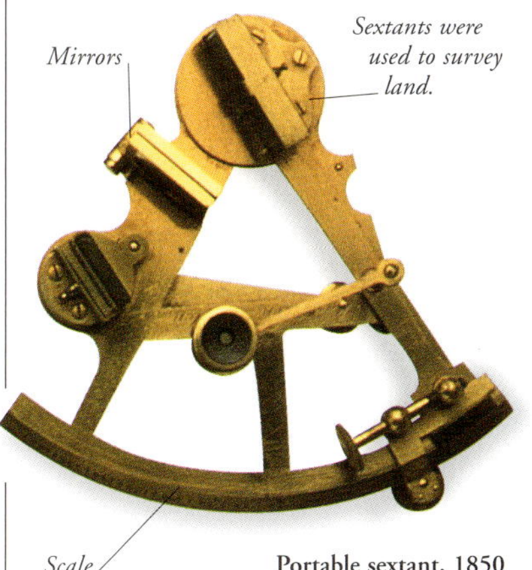

Mirrors

Sextants were used to survey land.

Scale

Portable sextant, 1850

Empire building

From the 15th century, the Spanish, Portuguese, Dutch, British, and French created huge empires outside Europe. After a nation's explorers, traders, and settlers had made links with an overseas territory, it might easily come under that nation's rule as a colony. Africa, Australia, parts of Asia, and the Americas were all colonized by Europeans at one time.

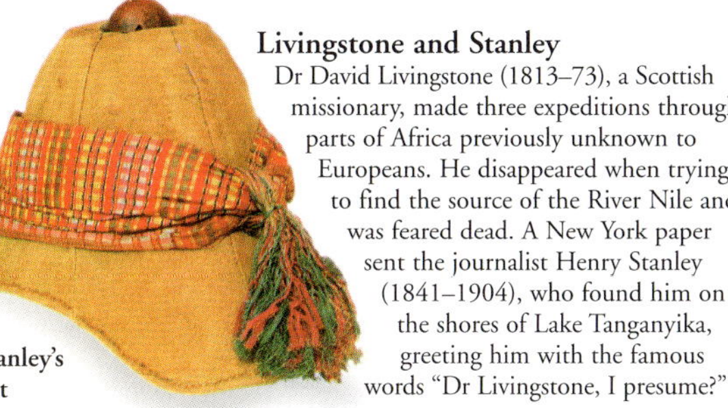

Livingstone and Stanley

Dr David Livingstone (1813–73), a Scottish missionary, made three expeditions through parts of Africa previously unknown to Europeans. He disappeared when trying to find the source of the River Nile and was feared dead. A New York paper sent the journalist Henry Stanley (1841–1904), who found him on the shores of Lake Tanganyika, greeting him with the famous words "Dr Livingstone, I presume?".

Stanley's hat

Charles Sturt

Despite the presence of two great rivers, the Murray and the Darling, Australian settlers could find no river mouths on the southeast coast, so explorers searched for an inland sea. In 1828–30, Sturt (1795–1869) mapped these river systems for 1600 km (994 miles). In 1844, he explored the Australian interior, or Outback, and finally proved there was no inland sea.

Final frontiers

In 1909 and 1911 the first-ever expeditions reached the North and South Poles. Since then there have been few places on Earth left to map but, with technological advances, scientists have been able to extend exploration to include investigations of the oceans and space. In 1969, explorers landed on the Moon for the first time.

Hubble Space Telescope

Astronomers can now explore time as well as space. The Hubble Space Telescope, launched in 1990, orbits Earth at a distance of 600 km (370 miles). From this distance it collects images travelling through space from millions of years ago.

Equipment box

Solar panel

Mary Kingsley

Few women took part in the first explorations of the world. It was generally believed that only men had the courage to venture into uncharted lands. However English naturalist Mary Kingsley (1862–1900) proved that this was untrue when she travelled through West Africa in 1893 and 1894, collecting fish and beetle specimens for the British Museum and studying African religions. In 1900 she returned to Africa to nurse soldiers in the Boer War, and died there.

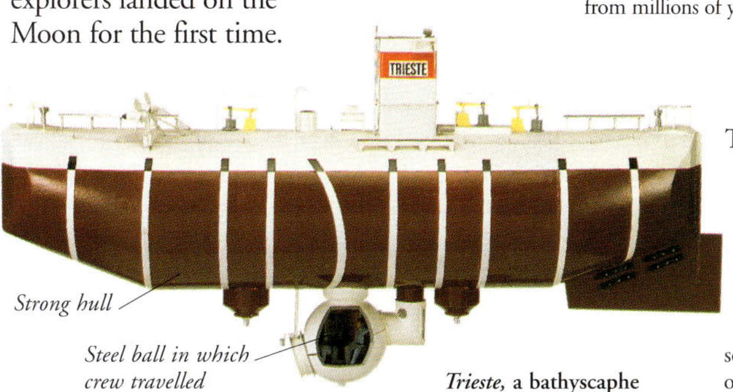

Strong hull

Steel ball in which crew travelled

Trieste, a bathyscaphe

Trieste submarine

The bathyscaphe, *Trieste* – a manned diving vessel designed to reach depths of up to 11 km (7 miles) in the ocean – was developed by the Swiss scientist Auguste Piccard (1884–1962). In 1960 it dived to a record 10,916 m (35,815 ft) in the Mariana Trench of the Pacific Ocean. On board were Piccard's son Jacques and Lieutenant Donald Walsh of the US Navy.

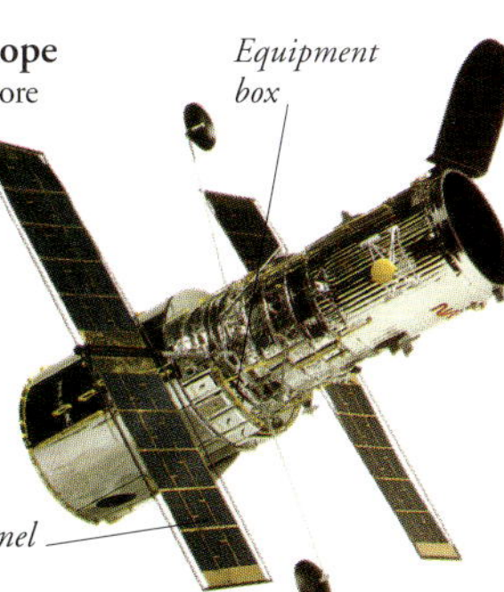

FIND OUT MORE   AUSTRALIA, HISTORY OF   ASIA, HISTORY OF   AFRICA, HISTORY OF   CENTRAL AMERICA, HISTORY OF   COOK, JAMES   EMPIRES   POLAR EXPLORATION   SOUTH AMERICA, HISTORY OF   SPACE EXPLORATION

EYES AND SEEING

YOUR EYES ENABLE you to see by stimulating the creation of images in your brain. Each of the two eyeballs is a sphere measuring 6.25 cm (2.5 inches) in diameter. Eyeballs contain sensory cells that, when stimulated by light, send messages to the brain that are interpreted as images. Reflex mechanisms control the amount of light entering the eye, and enable the eye to focus on objects whether they are near or distant. Much of the eyeball is hidden because it is protected within the orbit, a bony socket in the skull. The delicate outer surface of the eye is also protected by the eyelids.

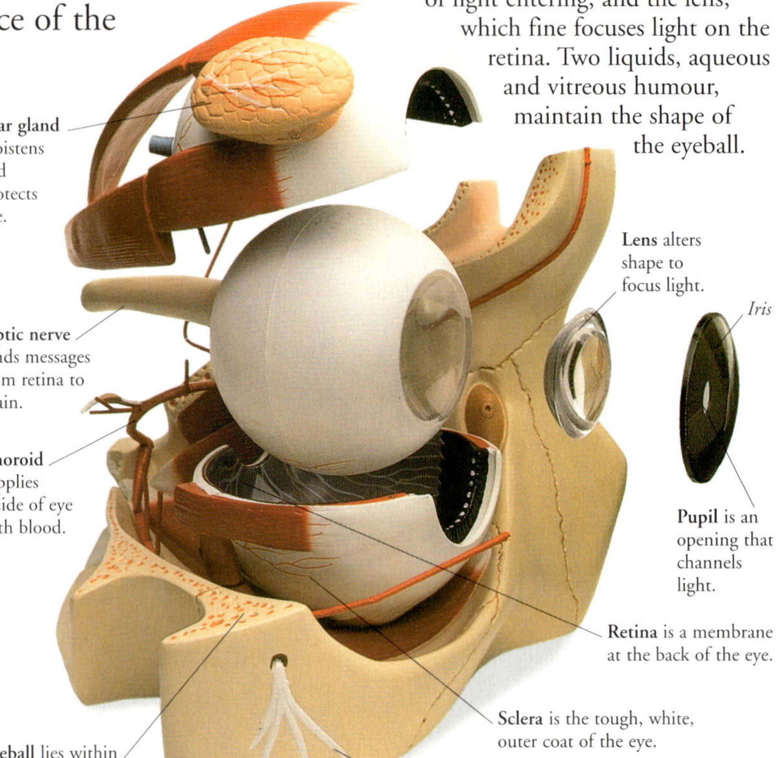

Moving the eye

Your eyes move constantly, even when you are staring. Six muscles move each eyeball and hold it in place inside its skull socket. Each muscle pulls the eye in a different direction, enabling the eyeball to move up and down, from side to side, and diagonally. Your brain controls these movements to make sure that both eyes move together.

Inside the eye

The transparent cornea at the front of the eye helps to focus light as it enters. Behind the cornea are the iris, which controls the amount of light entering, and the lens, which fine focuses light on the retina. Two liquids, aqueous and vitreous humour, maintain the shape of the eyeball.

Seeing

The eyes gather light from whatever you look at. The cornea and lens focus this light on the retina to produce an upside-down image. Cells inside the retina, called rods and cones, respond to light by sending nerve impulses along the optic nerve to the brain. The brain interprets these impulses so you see the image the right way up.

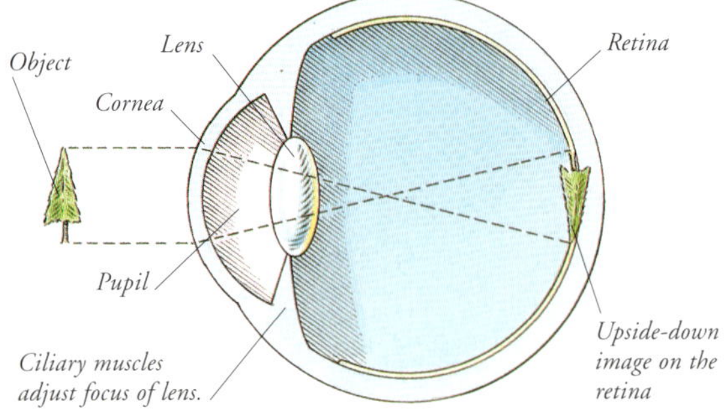

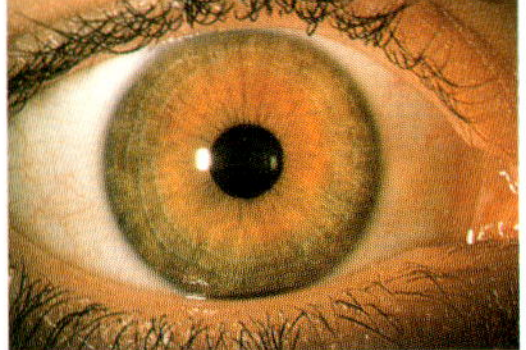

Iris and pupil

The iris controls the amount of light entering the eye. Muscles in the iris alter the size of the pupil, the opening that allows in light. In dim light, the pupil widens; in bright light, the pupil gets smaller.

Rods and cones

There are about 120 million rods and 7 million cones in the retina. Rods work best in dim light. Cones are responsible for colour vision and enable you to see things in detail.

Tears

Tears are released by lacrimal (tear) glands above the eye. When you blink, tears spread over the eye's surface. This keeps the cornea moist, washes away dust, and kills germs. After flowing over the eye, tears drain through two small openings at the side of the eye into the lacrimal duct, and then into the nose.

Vision defects

The most common vision problems are long sight and short sight. In both cases the eye does not focus light properly on the retina. Some people, mainly males, have colour blindness and cannot distinguish between certain colours, most often red and green.

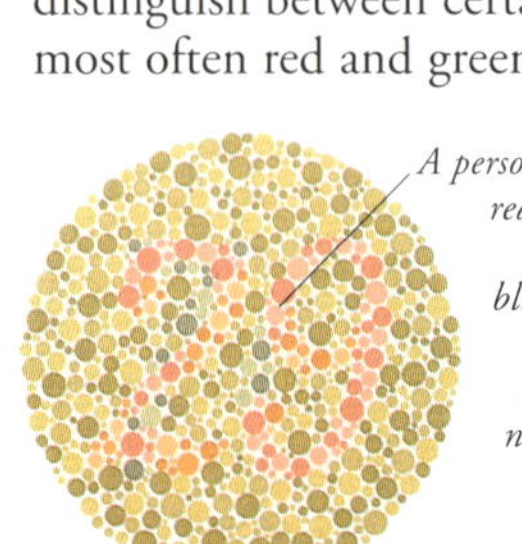

Long sight

A long-sighted person sees distant objects clearly, but has a blurred view of close objects. This happens because light from near objects is focused behind the retina, rather than on it.

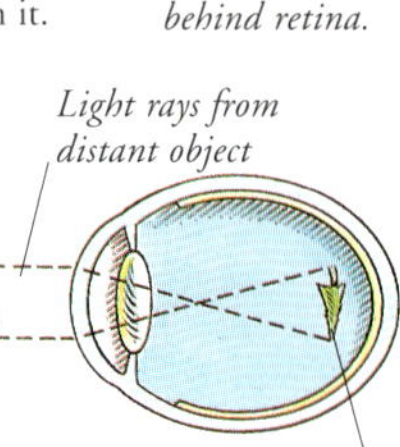

Short sight

A short-sighted person can see close objects clearly, but sees distant objects as a blur. Short sight is usually caused by the eyeball being longer than normal. This means that light entering the eye from distant objects is focused in front of the retina, rather than on it.

FIND OUT MORE — BRAIN AND NERVOUS SYSTEM · CAMERAS · CELLS · COLOUR · GENETICS · HUMAN BODY · LIGHT · MEDICINE, HISTORY OF

FARMING

BY CULTIVATING CROPS and raising animals, farms produce food and other products. Ten per cent of people in developed nations, and 60 per cent in developing countries, make their living from farming. In the West, technology makes the land highly productive, producing abundant, cheap food, and requiring fewer workers. In developing countries, farms have much lower yields because the soil or climate are often unsuitable for agriculture, and farmers, unable to afford new machines and chemicals, must rely on labour-intensive methods.

Crops

Ancient farmers bred crop plants by collecting and sowing the seed from the healthiest wild plants: the first cultivated crop was probably a kind of wheat. Today's major food crops are wheat, rice, maize (corn), and potatoes; major non-food crops include cotton and tobacco. The types and quantities of crops a farmer can grow are determined by soil and climate.

Cotton bolls (seed pods)

Cotton
The cotton crop provides fibres and oil. The main producers of the world's cotton are China and the USA.

Types of farms

In the developed world, mixed farms were once common; farmers grew a few different crops and kept some livestock. Today's technology makes it advantageous for farms to specialize, raising just one kind of crop or animal with very high output. Such farming is big business. Some farmers, concerned by the possible effects on the environment, have changed to organic farming, where artificial fertilizers and pesticides are not used.

Shepherd shakes seed pods from a tree to feed sheep.

Subsistence farming, Kenya

Subsistence farming
Subsistence farmers produce only enough to feed their household, with little or no surplus to sell. This is more common in developing nations where many farmers cannot afford the chemicals or machinery that would increase their yield, and rely on centuries-old farming methods.

Commercial farming
Commercial farmers farm animals and crops intensively. They aim for a high yield and sell their produce for profit. In many countries, farmers produce too much food. When surplus crops and animals force food prices down, damaging the food industry, governments pay farmers to grow less.

Cattle fair, Argentina

Rice
Rice is a cereal, and the main food of half the world's people. Asia produces 90 per cent of the world's crop. Plants are grown in warm climates, usually on flooded "paddy" fields. Rice is a labour-intensive crop, which means most of the work is done by people, rather than machines.

Harvesting rice by hand

Terraced fields

Rice seedlings

2 days old   *2–3 weeks*   *4–5 weeks*

Paddy field, China

Plants are cut down, and left in bundles to dry out.

Livestock

Farmers rear livestock (animals) for meat, milk, eggs, skins, and wool. In some cases, livestock is reared intensively, with many animals kept indoors in artificial conditions to encourage fast growth. By contrast "free-range" animals are reared outside; they live more like their wild counterparts, but their products are more costly.

Farmers kept goats and sheep for milk long before cattle.

Sheep's milk

Butter, from cow's milk

Cheese, from goat's milk

Dairy farming
Dairy farming is the breeding of animals for their milk and milk products. Cows are the main dairy animals, producing 10 to 15 litres (2.6 to 4 US gallons) of milk a day on average. Sheep and goats are also raised for their milk.

Sheep
The versatile sheep produces meat, wool, and milk. Sheep do not need such rich pasture as cattle: they can survive on poor quality land, and in dry or cold climates.

Sheep-shearing takes place in late spring.

Sorting the maize harvest, Ghana

Maize
Maize is a kind of grass. There are many varieties, which can be ground into flour, eaten as a vegetable, made into oil, or used as animal feed. Maize is a major crop in the United States, Brazil, southern Africa, and parts of Asia.

Maize

Farming technology

Ever since the Agricultural Revolution in the 18th century, scientific advances in agriculture have rapidly raised farms' productivity. Artificial fertilizers, pesticides, research into selective breeding, and genetic engineering keep the increasing Western populations fed. Selective breeding programmes improve crops and livestock by combining the strengths of each parent in their offspring. By modifying genes directly in the laboratory, scientists can achieve the same results as selective breeding in a fraction of the time.

Chemicals in farming

Fertilizers enrich the soil with the minerals essential for plant growth. Animal manure is an organic fertilizer; science has also developed inorganic (artificial) fertilizers. Pesticides are chemicals that control the pests which attack crops. While these chemicals improve productivity, some chemicals get into the water supply, possibly harming human health.

Vegetables can be bred to be regular in shape, and so more attractive to shoppers, even though there is no difference in taste.

Intensively farmed

Irregular shape

Cattle raised in zero-grazing pen

Intensive rearing

Intensive farming maximizes the production of crops and livestock with chemicals and machines. Shoppers prefer cheap food: to produce this, the cost of raising livestock must be kept to a minimum. Cattle, pigs, and other animals live in controlled conditions; for example, pigs live in units, and are fed a precise mix of nutrients that make them put on the most weight in the least time.

Machinery

During the 20th century, new machinery increased farm productivity in industrialized nations, while also cutting labour requirements. Tractors, motor vehicles that pull farm machinery, quickly replaced horses as the source of pulling power on the farm. The tractor's power allowed farmers to plant and harvest crops over vast areas.

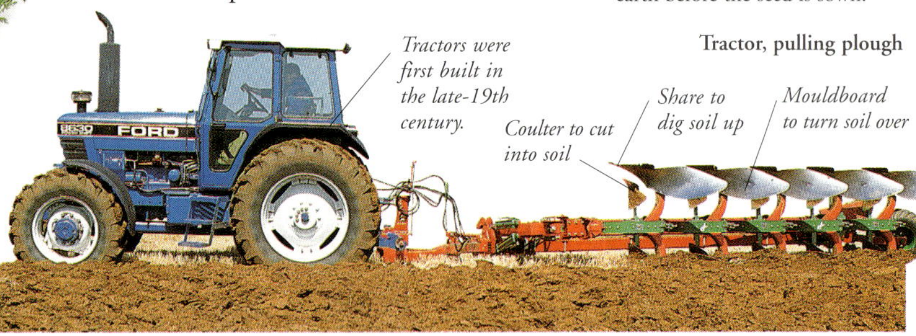

Tractors were first built in the late-19th century.

Coulter to cut into soil

Share to dig soil up

Mouldboard to turn soil over

Tractor, pulling plough

Because combine harvesters work so quickly, they reap a crop at its best.

Harvesters

Machines can speed the harvest. A combine harvester both cuts a crop of wheat and separates the grain from the stalk. In less than an hour, a machine with one driver can turn two hectares of wheat into grain. Sugar, potatoes, and peas are other crops harvested by machine.

Equipment

Milking machines have changed the face of dairy farms, with farmers now able to keep much larger herds of cattle. Farmers operate machines that milk cattle twice a day, although in the Netherlands robotic machines have been introduced that milk cows whenever the cows want it. The robots place vacuum cups on the cows' teats to draw out their milk. Each cow wears a radio collar which tells the robot where to look for the udder.

Preparing the land

To prepare the soil for sowing seed, farmers first plough the fields. The blade of a plough cuts a deep furrow in the soil and turns it over, burying weeds, which rot to enrich the soil. Harrows and cultivators are then used to break up large lumps of earth before the seed is sown.

Robotic milking parlour, the Netherlands

The farmer's year

The changing seasons set the pace of a farmer's work. On a livestock farm, for instance, spring is the time when lambs or calves are born. The arable (crop-growing) farm is busiest during the spring-to-autumn growing season. Apple growers must carry out different tasks through the year to produce the best crop.

Apples are the main fruit crop in cool, temperate regions. There are more than 6,000 different varieties.

Trees have been pruned so that the Sun can ripen the fruit.

To make mechanical weeding easier, the trees are grown in neat rows.

Winter: the trees take a rest from growing. The farmer prunes the branches into shapes that make the fruit easier to reach.

Farmer prunes trees.

Windfalls

Bees dust pollen from blossom of one tree to that of another.

Beehive

Modern apple trees have been bred to be small, making it easier for people to pick the fruit.

Tractor moves bins of picked apples.

Free-range pigs eat windfall apples.

Late summer: the fruits ripen at the end of summer, when harvest (by hand) begins.

Autumn: harvest continues. Windfalls are used to make cider and juice.

Spring: bees from hives placed in the orchard in spring pollinate the trees.

Trees are sprayed and fed in spring and summer.

FIND OUT MORE — FARMING, HISTORY OF · FISHING INDUSTRY · FOOD · GENETICS · INDUS VALLEY CIVILIZATION · PIGS AND PECCARIES · PLANT USES · SHEEP AND GOATS · SOIL · TRADE AND INDUSTRY

Farming

Animals farmed for produce

Chickens are bred for eggs and meat.

Peacocks are bred for their exotic plumage.

Ducks are farmed for feathers, eggs, and meat.

Sheep are bred for milk, meat, skins, and wool.

Geese are kept for meat, down, and eggs.

Red deer are bred for their meat, called venison.

Cattle are farmed for milk and meat.

Goats are farmed for milk, meat, and wool.

Ostrich chick: farmed for meat and feathers.

Saanen goats are bred in Europe for their milk.

Chinchillas, rodents bred for their soft, delicate fur.

Pigs are farmed for pork, bacon, other meat products, skins, and bristles.

Animals bred to work

Camels are used as pack animals, and also farmed for wool, milk, hides, and meat.

Heavy horses, used where a farmer has no tractor.

Donkeys carry large loads on little food or water.

Mules are interbred from horses and donkeys.

Elephants are used as draught (pulling) animals in southeast Asia.

FARMING, HISTORY OF

TEN THOUSAND YEARS AGO, the first farmers began to grow crops and breed animals for food. Before that, nomadic hunter-gatherers fed on berries, plants, and wild beasts they encountered on their travels. With the emergence of farming, however, people were able to produce a reliable food supply, and to settle permanently in one place, giving rise to the world's earliest civilizations in Mesopotamia, Egypt, India, and China. Farming methods continued to evolve slowly until, in the 18th century, a so-called Agricultural Revolution led to dramatic changes. Since then, farming has become more mechanized and feeds ever greater numbers of people.

Early farmers

The first farmers tamed wild animals, kept them in herds, and used them for meat, milk, skins, and wool. By contrast, nomadic herders moved their animals constantly in search of new pastures.

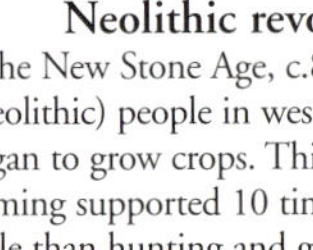
Flint sickle in wooden handle

Rice farming

Neolithic revolution

After the New Stone Age, c.8000 BC, (Neolithic) people in western Asia began to grow crops. This type of farming supported 10 times more people than hunting and gathering.

Irrigation

Early farmers needed water for their crops. Rivers and artificial canal systems played a vital role in the ancient agricultural civilizations of Egypt, the Indus Valley, and China.

Agricultural revolution

From about 1750, a series of major changes ushered in the era of modern farming. Key developments included large-scale farming, the intensive breeding of livestock, and the improvement of a number of agricultural techniques – such as four-course crop rotation – all of which were first developed in Britain.

Selective breeding

Robert Bakewell (1725–95), the fifth Duke of Bedford (1765–1802), and other British stock breeders during the Agricultural Revolution, used selective breeding on their farms and estates to develop larger, healthier animals, such as cattle, goats, sheep, and turkeys, with a higher milk or meat yield. Later breeders used the same system to develop animals for a particular purpose. For example, the Camargue bull which is bred only for fighting.

Goat

Camargue bull

Crop rotation

During the Agricultural Revolution, farmers found that if they grew certain crops, such as turnips, clover, barley, and wheat in successive years, they did not need to let the land lie fallow for a year. Root crops, such as turnips, improved the soil, and therefore the quality of the next harvest.

Turnips and wheat

Black Norfolk turkey

New farm machinery

Machines, such as the thresher (formulated in 1786 by Scots inventor Andrew Meikle), eased workloads and improved productivity. Threshers, which separated the grain from the straw, became more effective after 1850 when farm workers attached steam engines to power them.

Medieval farming

Farmers in medieval Europe divided the land around their village into three fields. Each family had one 12-hectare strip of land in each field. Everyone followed the same three-year farming cycle: one field was left fallow (unused) each year to restore the soil's nutrients, and the other two grew barley, oats, rye, or wheat.

Enclosures

From the 1500s, English landowners enclosed common land with fences, ditches or hedges, to turn it into private property. As a result, the co-operative medieval system of farming gave way to a system of private ownership where land-owners made all the decisions about what to farm.

Book of Hours, 1416

Charles "Turnip" Townshend

A main forerunner of the Agricultural Revolution, Viscount Townshend (1674–1738) retired from a brilliant career in politics to concentrate on farming. He popularized a four-course rotation of crops, and pioneered "marling" (using limey clay as fertilizer). His widespread cultivation of the turnip – as a fodder crop to keep animals fed during the winter – earned him his nickname.

Green Revolution

In the 1960s, a Green Revolution took place. New "high-yield" crop varieties were developed to increase wheat and rice production, particularly in highly populated countries such as India, and China. Critics claimed this process damaged the environment through overuse of fertilizer and concentration on only a few species. Recently farmers have been rediscovering traditional farming methods and using organic fertilizers and insecticides.

Steam-powered threshing machine

Seaweed, an organic fertilizer

FERNS

THE MOST ADVANCED of all the non-flowering, spore-bearing plants are the ferns and their relatives, known as the Pteridophytes. There are about 12,000 species of Pteridophyte, of which about 10,400 are ferns. The others include horsetails and club mosses. Pteridophytes are vascular plants, that is, plants whose stems contain tissues that transport water and food around the plant internally. They flourish best in warm, damp environments, but also grow where it is cool or dry.

Ferns

A typical fern plant has underground stems, or rhizomes, from which grow roots, and leaves called fronds. Upright rhizomes produce a fern with a short radiating crown of fronds, while long horizontal rhizomes produce a spreading fern. Ferns grow in a variety of places, but all have a two-stage life-cycle. The gametophyte is a small, short-lived plantlet that produces sex cells. After fertilization, a female sex cell grows into a sporophyte, which is the fern plant.

Epiphytic ferns

An epiphytic fern grows on the bough or trunk of a tree. It takes no nourishment from its host, but obtains moisture and minerals from rain and debris that become trapped among its roots.

Fronds hang clear of the branch.

Tree ferns

Tree ferns have woody, fibrous trunks topped with a crown of fronds. They are found in all climates, most frequently in the tropics and sub-tropics. The tallest species reaches 20 m (65 ft).

Radiating fronds

Base of dead fronds

Water ferns

Some ferns are aquatic. They either root into mud in fresh water, or float free. This *Azolla* species floats. Its tiny roots dangle in the water below a mat of fronds.

Male fern

Ferns similar to this male fern, so-called because of its vigorous growth, are found in woods all around the world. This species has stiff, bright green fronds. Each blade is divided into "leaves" called pinnae (singular: pinna), each of which is further divided into pinnules.

A full-grown frond may reach as much as 150 cm (5 ft) long.

Pinna and pinnules

The frond continues to lengthen as the lower parts unfurl.

Young frond

A developing male fern plant

Stipe is the "stalk" of the fern.

Rhizome

Root

1 Frond buds develop on the rhizome. Each bud produces just one frond. It takes up to three years for a bud to develop and a frond to start growing.

2 A frond can grow rapidly because all the cells of the stalk and leaflets are fully formed, though very small. They just have to expand.

3 A male fern produces tall fronds, each on a scaly stipe. Fertile fronds are the last to unfurl, so that the spores are released in the summer.

Club mosses

These small plants grow on damp ground or on rainforest trees. Their creeping stems are covered with tiny leaves arranged in a spiral. Spores are carried in modified leaves on fertile stems.

Horsetails

The stiff upright stems of horsetails grow in dense patches from underground stems. Branches are arranged in whorls, although fertile stems often have no branches. Tiny brown leaves grow in rings around the stems and branches. Spores are borne in cone-like structures on the tip of fertile stems.

Sterile stem

Fertile stem

The life-cycle of a fern

Sori

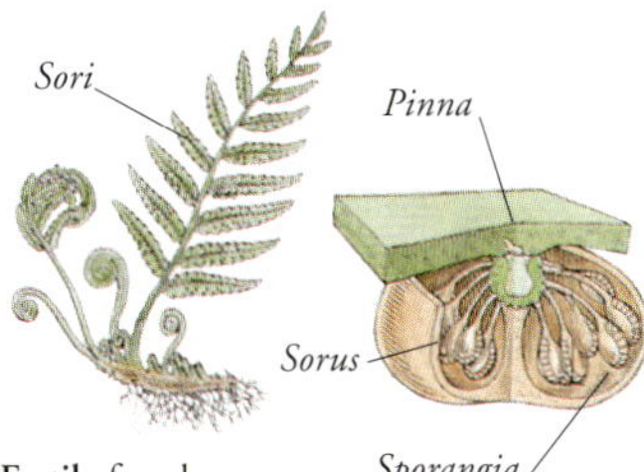

Pinna

Sorus

Sporangia

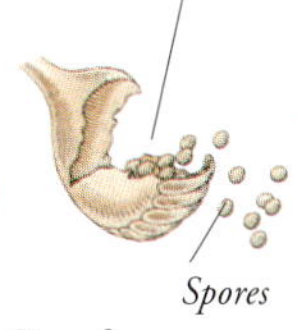

Dry weather causes the sporangium to burst at a weak spot.

Spores

Sex organs are carried on the underside of the gametophyte.

Gametophyte is a thin green plantlet.

Archegonium containing female sex cells

Antheridium containing male sex cells

New fern plant – the sporophyte

Fertile fronds have sori (singular: sorus), usually on the lower surface of each pinna.

Within each sorus are clusters of sporangia, which contain the spores.

Sixty-four spores develop inside each sporangium. The sporangium then bursts, releasing all the spores.

A spore landing on damp soil germinates into a gametophyte. This bears male and female sex organs.

Male sex cells swim in a film of soil moisture to the female sex cells and then fertilize them.

The first female sex cell to be fertilized grows into a fern plant.

FIND OUT MORE — MOSSES AND LIVERWORTS • PLANTS • PLANTS, ANATOMY • PLANTS, REPRODUCTION • RAINFOREST WILDLIFE • TREES

FESTIVALS

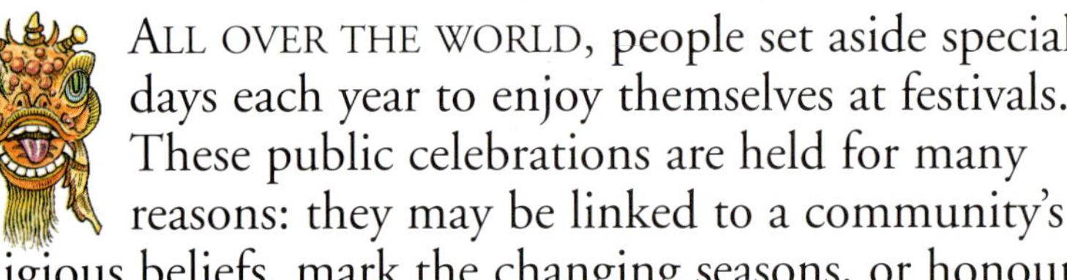

ALL OVER THE WORLD, people set aside special days each year to enjoy themselves at festivals. These public celebrations are held for many reasons: they may be linked to a community's religious beliefs, mark the changing seasons, or honour important events in a country's history.

Day of the Dead

On 1 November, Mexicans celebrate the Day of the Dead, to honour people who have died. Families have picnics by the graves of their relatives, decorate the streets with flowers and carved skeletons, and eat sweets shaped like skulls and coffins.

Papier-mâché skeleton

Calendar festivals

The majority of festivals are held at the same time each year. Many religions have adapted the celebrations of early peoples to their own ends: the Christian Christmas and the Hindu Diwali are held around the same time as ancient feasts marking the onset of winter.

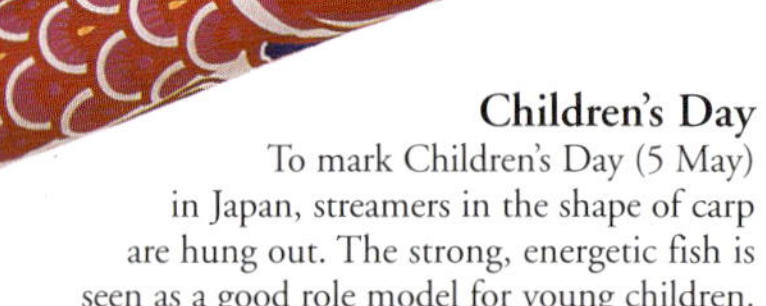
Children's Day
To mark Children's Day (5 May) in Japan, streamers in the shape of carp are hung out. The strong, energetic fish is seen as a good role model for young children.

Harvest festivals

Ancient peoples thought that thanking the gods would ensure a good crop the next year, and people still celebrate festivals based on this idea. There are many festivals in Africa and Papua New Guinea that celebrate the yam crop, and the Oktoberfest beer festival in Germany began as thanks for the crop of hops.

Radishes
On Christmas Eve, townspeople in Oaxaca, Mexico, celebrate their radish crop by carving large, recently harvested radishes into elaborate shapes, which they use to decorate market stalls and restaurants. Food is served on chipped plates, which are saved for the occasion and smashed at the end of the night.

Corn

In England, people often used the last of the year's corn to make a figure called a corn dolly. The dolly kept the corn spirit alive through the winter, ensuring another good harvest the next year.

Traditional English corn dolly

Carnivals

Originally, carnivals were pagan festivals to celebrate the rebirth of nature in spring. Later, they became associated with the Roman Catholic festival of Lent. The start and duration of the carnival season varies from country to country.

Carnival in Venice
This famous Italian carnival first began in the 11th century. Traditionally, many revellers wear masks. They originally did this to hide their faces while they behaved outrageously.

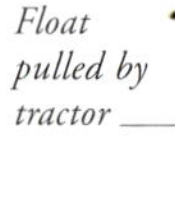
Float pulled by tractor

Mardi Gras float

Caribbean carnival
Carnival in the Caribbean combines African and European traditions; dance, costume, and music are important parts of African religious beliefs.

Mardi Gras

In many Roman Catholic countries, carnival is by tradition a last chance for merry-making before the start of Lent, the weeks of fasting that come before Easter. Thousands of people enjoy the week-long Mardi Gras carnival in New Orleans, USA, which is named after the French for "Fat Tuesday". This refers to Shrove Tuesday, the day before Lent begins, when all the fats in the home must be used up. Another spectacular Mardi Gras carnival is held in Rio de Janeiro, Brazil.

Modern festivals

Most festivals set up today mark non-religious events. The Olympics celebrate excellence in sports; the Edinburgh festival in the UK promotes the performing arts.

Mime artist, Edinburgh Festival

Roskilde
Thousands of fans attend this summer rock music festival in Denmark.

Political festivals

Significant political dates are often the cause for regular celebration. Festivals mark the anniversary of a nation's independence or a great leader's birthday: in the USA, there is a holiday on George Washington's birthday.

May Day
Once a springtime fertility festival, May 1 is a now a public holiday to honour workers. In Russia, May Day is marked with trades union parades.

FIND OUT MORE   CHRISTIANITY   FILMS AND FILM-MAKING   FOOD   HINDUISM   SPORT   UNIONS, TRADE

FEUDALISM

IN PARTS OF MEDIEVAL ASIA and Europe, a system arose for organizing society known as feudalism. In the feudal system, the king gave land to powerful barons, who then gave land and protection to lesser lords, and so on through to the peasants. Each level was expected to fight to protect its overlords whenever needed. European feudalism started in the 9th century, and spread over the continent. Outside Europe, the feudal system operated in Palestine during the Crusades, and also in Japan, where samurai gave military service to their overlords in return for land.

Lords and vassals

In the European feudal system, the only person who owned land was the king. When the king granted land to a baron, the baron pledged to be the king's vassal (servant). Lesser lords swore a similar oath to the barons and became their vassals, and peasants swore allegiance to the lords. Bishops were also the king's vassals, and held nearly as much power as the barons.

Feudal counsel
Kings and barons often asked for advice, or counsel, from their vassals when making any important decisions. This 14th-century French manuscript shows Philip VI of France judging Robert of Valois, helped by the bishops on his right hand and the barons on his left.

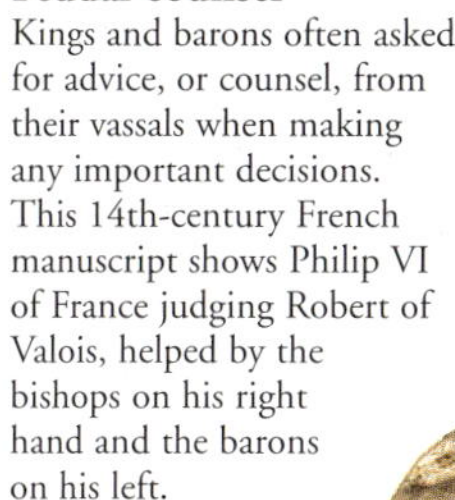

Feudal contract
The people owed their loyalty to the monarch. This "contract" meant that Philip VI could – and did – tax his subjects heavily to finance the Hundred Years War.

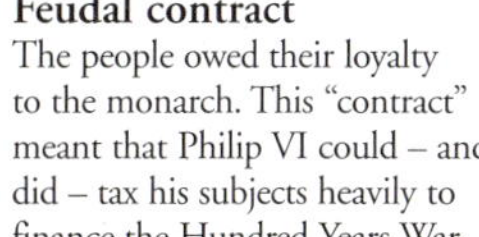

Domesday Book

For the feudal system to work well, the ruler needed detailed information about the land and who lived on it. William of Normandy, who introduced feudalism to Britain, had a complete record made of all land ownership in England in 1085–86. This became known as the Domesday Book.

The book is the most complete record of land-holding in medieval Europe.

How feudalism began

The great emperor Charlemagne insisted that all his nobles swear loyalty to him. This bond beween lord and warrior began the feudal system. Over the next two centuries, feudalism spread through France, Germany, northern Italy, the Slav countries, and finally the British Isles and Sicily.

Mounted warriors
Warriors riding horses to war became more common after 950. These warriors were the first knights. They had great prestige, and became an important part of the feudal system.

Derisive image of king with cat, not crown, on his head

King
Although the king owned the land, he could rarely afford to keep an army. He was often in conflict with the barons, on whom he relied for his warriors.

Barons
The most powerful of all the nobles, the barons got their lands directly from the king. Because they provided the royal army, they had great power and prestige.

Local lords
Local knights got their land (or manor) from the barons. In return, they fought for the barons when needed. As time went on, local lords often paid a tax called scutage (shield money) instead of fighting, and the king used this money to hire professional soldiers. In peacetime, they farmed and kept order.

Peasants
The peasants, at the bottom of feudal society, got their plots of land from the local lord of the manor. He allowed them to farm this land; in return, they paid rent in produce and money. The peasants also contributed several days' labour on public projects such as road- and bridge-building.

The manor

Farmland and its ownership was the most important part of feudalism, and the manor was the administration centre of the system. The lands surrounding the manor house were divided into the demesne (for the lord's own use), the arable (granted in parcels to the peasants), and the meadow lands (used by everyone for livestock).

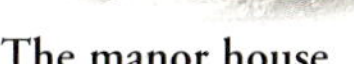

Ightham Mote, England

The manor house
Every manor house had a hall. This acted as the dining and living room for the family, and also a general reception room where the peasants paid their rent. The kitchen was at one end of the hall, beside a pantry and buttery (store room for drinks). Buildings in the courtyard included workshops and cattle-sheds. The whole complex was often surrounded by a moat for protection.

The Hall, Ightham Mote

William I

The illegitimate son of Duke Robert I of Normandy, William (c.1028–1087) conquered England in 1066. He introduced the feudal system to the island, and replaced Saxon nobles with Norman lords.

FIND OUT MORE   CHARLEMAGNE   HUNDRED YEARS WAR   KNGHTS AND HERALDRY   MEDIEVAL EUROPE   NORMANS   SAMURAI AND SHOGUNS

FILMS AND FILM-MAKING

IN 1895, THE Lumière brothers held the first public film screening, in a room below a Parisian café. The black and white images flickered on a silent screen, yet the audience was enthralled. The magic of the movies has continued ever since. Technology developed rapidly: sound arrived in 1927, colour in the 1930s, and today's complex films often involve stunning special effects. Film production is now an international industry, generating great wealth and employing thousands worldwide.

Casting

It is vital to the success of a movie to cast (place) actors who suit their parts artistically. Audiences have their favourites, so the choice of a popular star can turn a promising film into a huge box-office success.

Pre-production

Film-making begins long before the cameras start to turn. After a studio (a film-making company) agrees to make a movie, a script is prepared, the budget drawn up, actors and skilled crew hired, and the entire production planned to the last detail.

The producer

A producer decides which film to make, finds the money to finance it (often millions of pounds), and brings together the stars, script, and director.

Storyboard

Pictures represent each shot.

With one small picture for each shot, a storyboard is important in planning a film and gives an idea of what it will look like. Notes outline the action and dialogue.

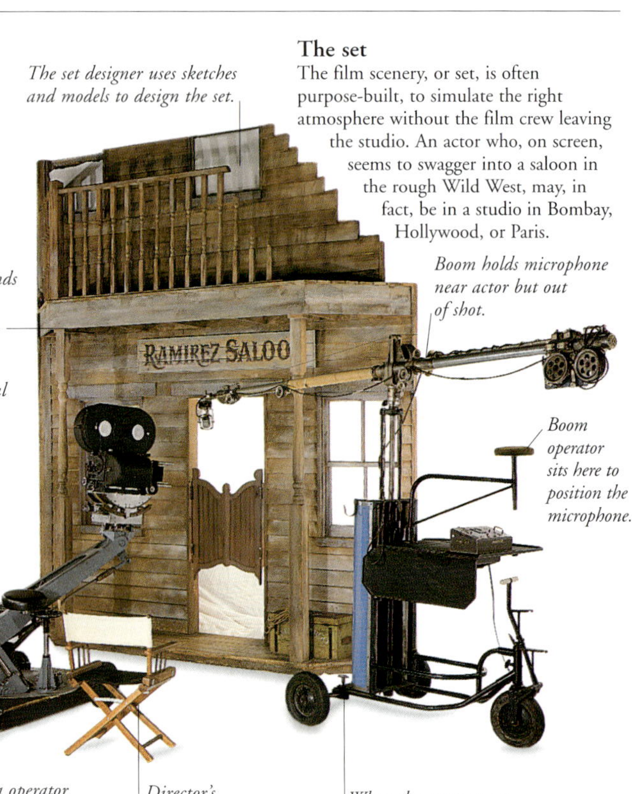

Focus puller has a seat at top of crane to adjust the focus on the camera lens.

The set designer uses sketches and models to design the set.

The set

The film scenery, or set, is often purpose-built, to simulate the right atmosphere without the film crew leaving the studio. An actor who, on screen, seems to swagger into a saloon in the rough Wild West, may, in fact, be in a studio in Bombay, Hollywood, or Paris.

The set decorator finds props and decorates set.

Boom holds microphone near actor but out of shot.

Powerful light

Boom operator sits here to position the microphone.

Crane raises the camera above the actors' heads.

The camera and camera equipment on set are moved by the grip.

The camera operator sits here to work the camera during shooting.

Director's folding chair next to camera

When the actors move, grips push the stand to move the microphone.

Production

When filming begins, a movie set is crowded with equipment, and each piece is the responsibility of a specific member of the crew. Between takes (sequences of filming), everyone works frantically to ensure that everything is adjusted exactly as the director wants. Off the set, props, wardrobe, and make-up have their own staff on hand.

The director

Responsible for the artistic side of the film-making process, the director is the most important person on set. Directors control the action and judge how well each take brings the script to life. They consult with experts in each department, such as the director of photography, who is responsible for the way the film looks.

Screen to view the film

Loudspeaker plays back sound track

Editing table

Motion pictures

The continuous action on a movie screen is, in fact, an illusion. What we are watching are thousands of still photographs, taken rapidly one after the other. A film camera shoots 24 photographs (frames) every second, and when the images are projected at the same rate, our eyes merge the pictures together. Over 27 m (90 ft) of film is shot for just one minute of cinema.

Post-production

Separate scenes in a film are shot in whatever order suits the crew. Then the director chooses the best sections, and the film editor links them in the right sequence to tell the story. While working closely with the director and other technicians, the editor carefully aligns the sound track and pictures, and adds the special effects.

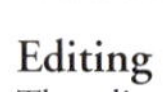

Editing

The editor cuts up the disjointed sequences of film, cutting between frames, and splices them together. Cuts are viewed at an editing table.

Sound track

Music, the actors' speech, and any background sound effects are each recorded separately and then combined to make the sound track.

Types of films

From the simplest short cartoon film to a full-length feature with an all-star cast, films cover every subject. There have been notable films on many topics, but some of the most successful movies have been in areas where film can add an extra dimension, such as the vivid settings of fantasy and space adventures or western movies, the special effects of science-fiction and horror films, or the singing and dancing of American musicals.

Babe, 1995

Babe is a piglet who believes he is a sheepdog.

Comedy
The first films were silent, yet the comic antics of the actors made audiences roar with laughter. Today, comedies range from biting social commentaries to the gentle humour of an animal film such as *Babe*.

Charlie Chaplin
One of the best-loved comedians of the silent screen, Chaplin (1889–1977) moved to the USA from London as a young man. He appeared in over 60 short films and 11 full-length comedies, including *City Lights* and *Modern Times*. His characterization of a tramp, who keeps a sense of humour despite great hardship, was based on observation of poor people on the London streets.

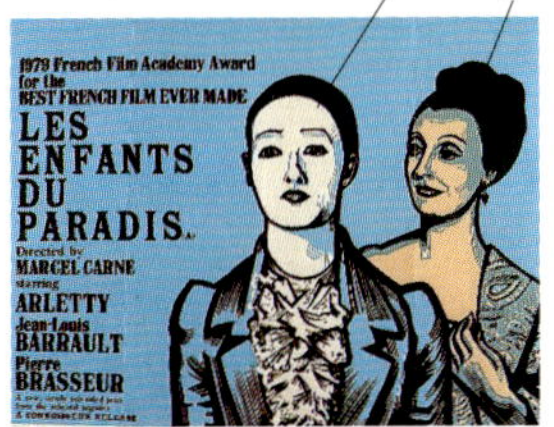
Les Enfants du Paradis, 1944

Jean-Louis Barrault   Arletty

Romance
Love stories are always popular. The romantic *Les Enfants du Paradis* was made in German-occupied France during World War II; in 1979, French critics voted it the best French film ever made.

Horror
German film makers were the first to realise that audiences like being frightened: directors were making horror movies in Germany by 1913. By the 1930s, horror had caught on in Hollywood, where it has been popular ever since. *Frankenstein* appeared in 1931. More than 100 films have been based on the same theme since.

Boris Karloff as Frankenstein's monster

Going to the movies

By the 1930s, going to the cinema was popular entertainment, but in the 1950s television took over and the film industry declined. Recently, movie-going has grown popular again. Today, multiplex cinemas screen many films at the same time, offering audiences a wide choice of pictures.

Special effects

Anything can happen on film, thanks largely to the special effects department, a complex and skilled area of film-making. Effects may range from animals that seem to talk, to horrific dripping wounds, or people appearing to fly through the air.

Dog, from The Storyteller

Eyes, nose, and mouth operated by motors.

Motor

Make-up
Actors wear make-up to look natural under the bright film lights. Make-up also helps when an actor must look unnatural. A make-up artist can make an actor look much older, or use latex rubber and lining colours to add dreadful wounds. In horror and science-fiction films, make-up is used to turn people into aliens.

Make-up in Terminator 2

Movie models
Where it is too costly, dangerous, or impossible to use the real thing, film-makers may turn to models. Tiny models stand in for massive spacecraft in science-fiction films. A talking animal may be a puppet, or an actor in costume whose remote-controlled mask is operated by a puppeteer. This kind of puppetry is called animatronics.

Blue screen
To create the illusion that a character is flying, an actor is filmed in front of a blue screen. Wind machines make his clothes flutter, as if air is moving past. An optical printer then combines the sequence with footage shot from a plane, or of a simulated space environment. The printer re-photographs images from each film onto a single frame, to blend the two films seamlessly.

Actor held by wires

Computers
Computers can manipulate images to create extraordinary special effects. Programs also allow operators to draw and animate characters on screen. Changes are much easier to make here than in animation which has been hand-drawn frame by frame.

Disney's Toy Story *is a computer-generated film.*

© Disney

Le Grand Rex cinema, Paris, France

Dramatic lighting

Picture palaces
Following the arrival of sound in 1927, cinemas were built in most towns in North America, Europe and Australia. With their impressive architecture, the cinemas of the 1920s and 1930s were often called picture palaces.

Neon sign

Hype and merchandise
The cost of film production means it is vital to make the public eager to see a movie, so that the producers can earn back their investment and make a good profit. Publicists work hard to sell a film before it opens. They inform journalists, and arrange for the actors to appear on television talk shows. This process is known as hype. Selling items related to a movie, such as socks or a mug, is another way of making more money.

Batman logo

Batman merchandise
™ & © 1996 DC Comics

Timeline

Academy Award (Oscar)
© A.M.P.A.S. ®

1895 The Lumière brothers open the first public cinema in Paris, France.

1913 By this date, Hollywood, Calif., is the centre of the US film industry.

1920s Russian director Sergei Eisenstein (1898–1948) introduces cross-cutting, showing bursts of action one after the other so they seem to happen simultaneously.

1927 The Academy of Motion Picture Arts and Sciences is set up; in 1929, it honours film-makers for the first time.

1927 *The Jazz Singer,* made in the US, is the first full-length film with sound.

1932 The "three-strip" process is introduced by the Technicolor company, and colour films, originally developed much earlier, begin to take off.

Technicolor three-strip camera

1941 US actor-director Orson Welles (1915–85) releases *Citizen Kane;* it explores new techniques in lighting, dialogue, and the use of camera lenses.

1952 The CinemaScope process introduces wide-screen cinema.

1960s *Nouvelle Vague* ("New Wave") film-makers in France introduce influential new techniques.

1980s The VCR allows people to see films at home.

1990s Special effects techniques are advanced.

FIND OUT MORE   CAMERAS   CARTOONS AND ANIMATION   EDISON, THOMAS   VIDEO

Film posters

United States

The Gold Rush (USA, 1925), a classic silent film, is touching yet very funny.

Raging Bull (USA, 1980) is one of the most influential films of the 1980s.

Blade Runner (USA, 1982) portrays a bleak Los Angeles in 2019.

Do the Right Thing (USA, 1989) develops from comedy to social comment.

Europe

The Battleship Potemkin (USSR, 1925), commissioned by Soviet leaders to put across a powerful political message, is still referred to as a masterpiece of cinema.

Metropolis (Ger. 1926) is a disturbing vision of an "ideal" city in the year 2000.

Pelle the Conqueror (Den/Swe. 1987) won top international awards.

Oceania

Once Were Warriors (NZ, 1994): a great success critically and at the box-office.

Four Weddings and a Funeral (UK, 1994) is a light-hearted, appealing romance.

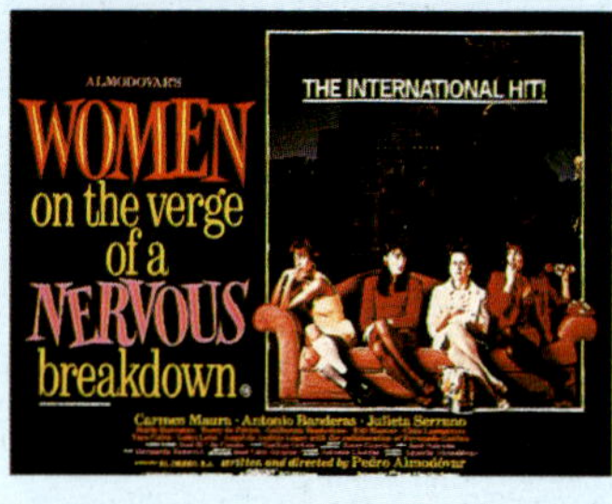

Women... (Spain, 1988) is a manic farce from talented director Pedro Almodóvar.

The Piano (Aust. 1993), directed and written by Jane Campion, won three Oscars.

Africa

Yeelen (Mali, 1987) tells the story of the struggle between a father and son.

The Sixth Day (Egypt, 1986), directed by Youssef Chahine, starred actress Daleeda.

In **Yaaba** (Burkina, 1989), a friendship develops between a boy and an old woman cast out by other villagers.

Asia

Ran (Japan, 1985) is based on *King Lear* by Shakespeare; the battle scenes are superbly staged and shot.

Pather Panchali (India, 1956) brought its director, Satyajit Ray, world recognition.

Raise the Red Lantern (HK, 1991) looks at a woman's life in 1920s' China.

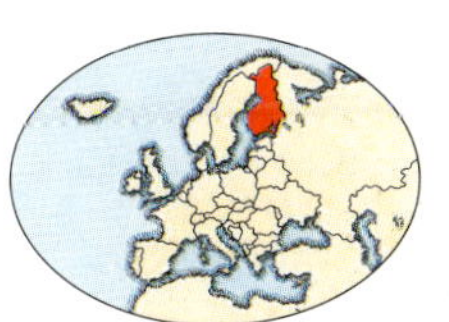

FINLAND

A LAND OF LAKES AND FORESTS, Finland is bordered by Russia to the east, the Baltic Sea to the south, and Sweden and Norway to the west and north. Finland shares government of Lapland, in the Arctic Circle, with Sweden and Norway. Finland was ruled by Russia until 1917, and, as a result, Finns have more in common culturally with the east than with their Scandinavian neighbours. A wealthy, liberal nation, Finland was the first European country to give women the vote.

Physical features

From the air, Finland is a patchwork of lakes, peat bogs, and trees. Forests dominate the land, and water covers about ten per cent of the country. There are some 98,000 islands within the lakes, and 30,000 off the coast. The Arctic north, including part of Lapland, is a bleak area of rocky tundra.

Forests

Pine, spruce, and birch trees cover 80 per cent of Finland, making it the ninth most forested country in the world. The forest is most dense just south of the Arctic Circle and is often covered in snow.

Lakes and islands

Finland has more than 60,000 lakes, mainly in the southeast, carved out by glaciers in the last Ice Age. Many islands are scattered in the lakes and off the warm southwest coast, including 6,000 of the Åland Islands.

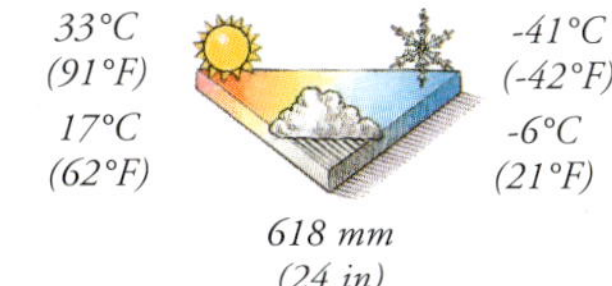

Climate

Finland has short, bright summers and long, cold winters when lakes often freeze up to 1 m (3 ft 3 in) deep. The Arctic north sees midnight sun in its 73-day summer.

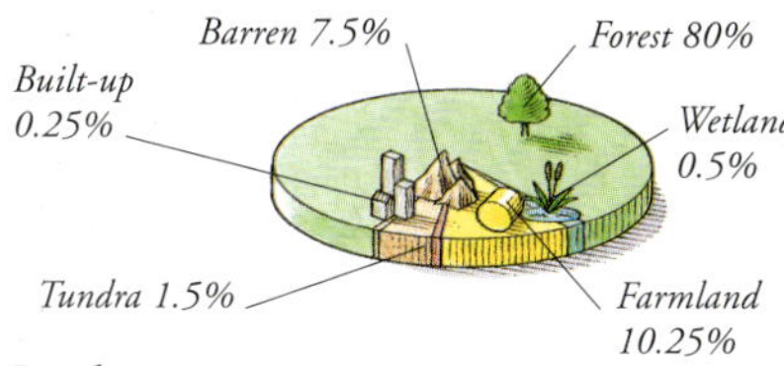

Land use

Dense forests and a maze of lakes, rivers, and peat bogs mean only 11 per cent of Finland's land can be used for crops or grazing animals. Despite this, farmers produce all of the country's dairy foods. The forests support a valuable timber industry, and the waters are used for fishing and hydroelectric power.

People

Almost half of the population lives around Helsinki. Families are close-knit, and most homes have a sauna, or hot, steamy relaxation room. Women enjoy equal rights and about 50 per cent pursue a career.

Cooling off after the sauna

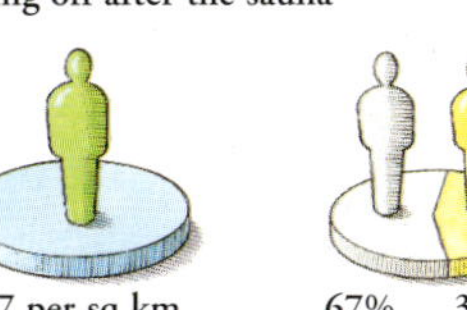

Kirkniemi paper mill

Farming and industry

Finland produces all of its own food. Most crops are grown in the southwest and on the sunny Åland Islands. The country is a world leader in the production of plywood, wood pulp, and paper, and these alone make up 30 per cent of the total exports. Furniture and high-tech manufacturing compete in world markets and, with the service sector, employ the majority of the work-force.

Helsinki

Standing on a peninsula and several islands in the Gulf of Finland, the vibrant capital of Helsinki has about 770,000 inhabitants. Tree-lined avenues and a colourful market back onto a busy harbour. Only half of the city's area has been developed, leaving parkland for the residents to enjoy.

The bustling Helsinki harbour

FIND OUT MORE   ARCTIC OCEAN   ENERGY   EUROPE, HISTORY OF   FISHING INDUSTRY   FORESTS   GLACIATION   LAKES   PAPER   SCANDINAVIA, HISTORY OF   TRADE AND INDUSTRY   WINTER SPORTS

FIRE

BURNING OUT OF CONTROL in forests or cities, a fire leaves a trail of destruction. Yet life without the benefits of fire is unimaginable. We use fire in power stations, car engines, and kitchens, to provide electricity and transport, or to cook food. Early humans realized the value of fire about half a million years ago – perhaps when lightning set a tree on fire. Learning to control and use the flames helped them hunt, clear land for farming, survive in colder climates, and eat foods that were inedible when raw. No wonder some religions still worship fire as a hungry god.

Flame is a glowing gas, produced in burning.

Combustion or burning

Fire is the heat and light produced when fuel burns. This process is known as combustion. The fuel can be any flammable material (one that can catch fire). The material must first be heated to a temperature called the ignition temperature; above this, it will burst into flame. As a fire gets hotter, more fuel catches alight, and the flames spread. Gases and vapours burn quickly; liquids and solids take longer to burn.

Using fire

To make fire do useful work, the supply of air or fuel must be controlled to keep the flames burning evenly. Furnaces, cooking stoves, and power plants use fire for the heat energy it produces. Heat is not always the main purpose of creating fire. In a car engine fuel burns explosively. Expanding gases drive the vehicle; the heat produced is wasted.

Welder at work

Welding

Many industrial processes rely on combustion. In the welder's torch, oxygen and acetylene gas mix and produce a flame hot enough to melt steel.

Fire-engine with hydraulic platform, used to reach awkward spaces.

Cooking

Many foods must be cooked before they can be eaten. When food is heated, chemical changes take place that improve its taste and make it easier to digest. Early people ate raw food until they discovered cooking, probably by accident.

Some booms are up to 62 m (203 ft) long.

Rescue platform

Arm, or boom

Built-in hose

Leg for support

Making a fire

In the past, there were two main methods of starting a fire: raising the temperature until flames appeared, or striking sparks to set light to tinder. Cigarette lighters still start fires by using the spark of flint on steel.

Mouthpiece steadies drill

Wooden drill

String

Modern model of bow drill

Hearth

Bow drills

Rapidly turning the string of a bow drill causes friction at the tip, which starts flames.

Tinder stored in box

Lid with candle holder

Steel

Flint

A tinder box contains flint, which makes sparks when struck against metal (the steel).

Piston handle is pumped to compress air.

A fire piston works like a bicycle pump: compressing air in the tube raises the temperature until the tinder (flammable material) inside catches alight.

Matches

Invented in 1827, these wooden splinters were tipped with chemicals. The chemicals were ignited by heat, generated by rubbing the tip against sandpaper. Safety matches burn only when rubbed against a specially coated strip on the matchbox.

Cooking with fire

Fighting fire

Fires feed on fuel, air, and heat; removing any one of these puts out the flames. Firefighters spray a blaze with water to remove heat and to create a blanket of steam that chokes off the air supply.

Myths about fire

The power and danger of fire made ancient peoples wonder about its origin. Myths that explain how people learned to tame flames occur in many separate cultures. Most fire myths involve a hero who brings fire to the world.

Prometheus

In Greek mythology, the chief god, Zeus, hid the secret of fire from mortals (humans) to punish them for a trick that a lesser god, Prometheus, had played on him. But Prometheus snatched a glowing ember from the Sun, and brought fire to the Earth.

Prometheus

FIND OUT MORE   FOOD   HEAT AND TEMPERATURE   INVENTIONS   LIGHT   PREHISTORIC PEOPLE

FIRST AID

FIRST AID RANGES from cleaning a small wound and covering it with sticking plaster, to dealing with serious injuries at a major disaster. But its main aims are the same: to save life, prevent the casualty's condition from worsening, promote healing and recovery, and arrange for expert help at the earliest opportunity. Recently, first aid has advanced greatly due to a better understanding of the body's needs in serious injury or disease, improved medical equipment, and mobile communications. It now plays an even more vital role in saving lives, and speeding a casualty's recovery.

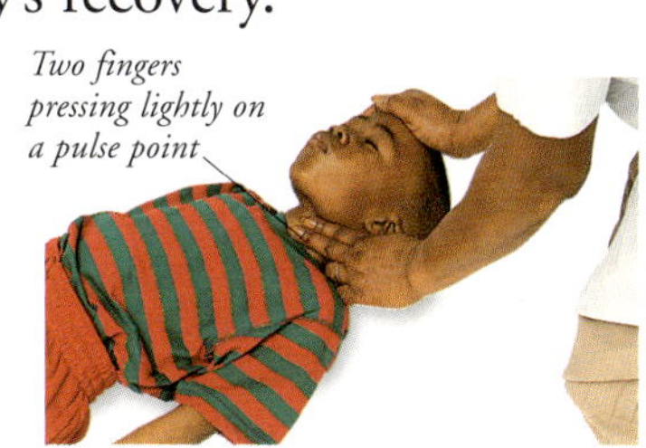
Scene of a motorcycle accident

At the scene

Effective first aid – the temporary treatment of injury or illness while waiting for medical aid – relies on correctly assigning priorities. At an accident, one of the first priorities is to summon the emergency services.

Assessing conditions
Experienced first aiders know that noisy casualties are not necessarily the most hurt. At a multiple accident, they assess quickly the condition of all casualties, then concentrate available first aid on the most seriously injured. In hospitals, this assessment is known as triage.

Spanish public telephone

Raising the alarm
A telephone call is usually the best way to get help. Special telephones are located in areas such as motorways, but calls to the emergency services are free on all telephones. Shouting, waving flags, or firing flares are all alternative methods.

Further danger
First aiders should never place themselves or others in danger. Before treating the casualty, they should try to make the area safe. Fire, traffic, electricity, and unsafe structures are some of the hazards that may delay treatment.

Fire extinguisher

ABC of first aid

ABC stands for the body's three vital needs. "A" stands for airway: the airway needs to be open so that oxygen-containing air can enter the lungs. "B" stands for breathing, by which the body inhales fresh air and expels stale air. "C" stands for the circulation of the blood, which distributes oxygen around the body. When dealing with an unconscious casualty, the first aider must check that the casualty has a clear airway, is breathing, and has a pulse that indicates blood circulation.

Two fingers pressing lightly on a pulse point

Checking for a pulse
The heart pumps blood around the body, causing a pulse. A first aider can check the heart is still beating by feeling for this pulse in arteries located in the neck or wrist.

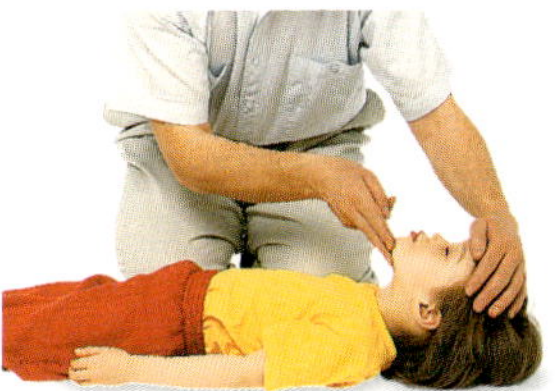

Airway
Inhaled foreign bodies or fluid can block the airway. By tipping the head back and straightening the airway, a first aider can look for blockages.

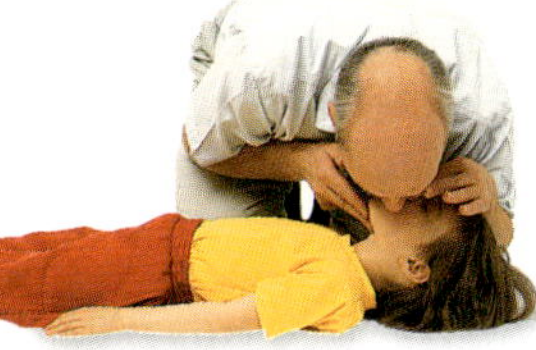

Breathing
If breathing stops, the first aider may blow air at regular intervals through the casualty's mouth into their lungs. This is called artificial ventilation.

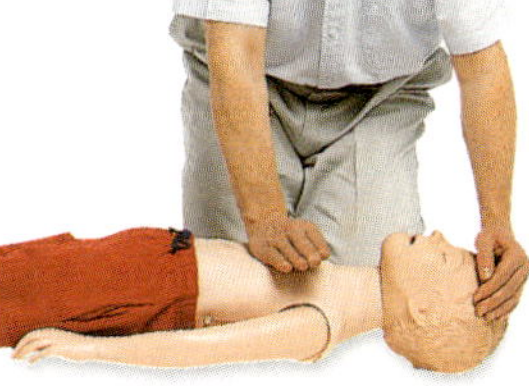

Circulation
If a pulse is absent, the first aider may carry out heart massage (external chest compression) to try to stimulate the heart into action.

First-aid kit

In many countries, the law requires workplaces and schools to keep first-aid kits. The contents should be kept in a clean, marked container and be re-stocked regularly. Because there is a danger of misusing drugs, the contents of some kits are restricted to sterile wound dressings.

Bent leg and arm in front of body prevent casualty rolling onto front.

An extended head and neck keeps the airway open and prevents the tongue blocking throat.

Recovery position

Recovery position
If the casualty is breathing but unconscious, the first aider may gently place him or her in the recovery position until expert help arrives. However, it is important to remember that a person involved in a bad accident may have damage to bones and nerves. First aiders should avoid moving the casualty, unless it is vital to save life.

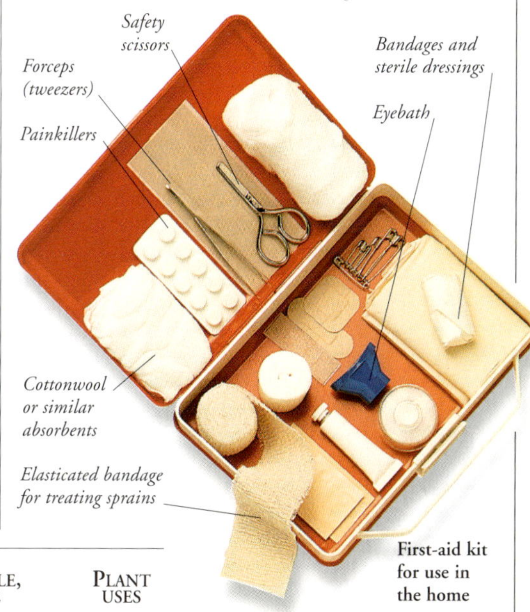

Safety scissors

Forceps (tweezers)

Painkillers

Bandages and sterile dressings

Eyebath

Cottonwool or similar absorbents

Elasticated bandage for treating sprains

First-aid kit for use in the home

FIND OUT MORE DRUGS HOSPITALS MEDICINE MEDICINE, HISTORY OF NIGHTINGALE, FLORENCE PLANT USES

FISH

THE FIRST FISH appeared in the seas 470 million years ago. Today, more than 20,000 species have been described, ranging from the great whale shark to the pygmy goby. Fish live in freshwater streams, rivers, and lakes, and in saltwater seas and oceans. A few, including eels and salmon, migrate from salt to fresh water. Some fish are fierce predators, and because of this many others have evolved a range of methods of defence. Although most fish leave their eggs and young to look after themselves, some species protect their young.

Fins
Most fish have a dorsal fin, paired pectoral and pelvic fins, and a tail for movement. In some fish, fins have become specialized as lifting foils, walking legs, suckers for holding on, or poisoned spines for protection.

Scales
Most fish have a covering of backward-facing scales that help to streamline them. Bony fish have either flat, oval, or square overlapping scales, while sharks have tooth-like structures buried in the skin.

Dorsal fin

Caudal, or tail, fin

Operculum (gill cover)

Pectoral fin   **European carp**

Anal fin

Pelvic fin

Fish features
Fish have a number of features in common. They breathe through gills, and are generally streamlined in shape with paired body muscles along each side. They have a tail for propulsion, fins for steering, and scales for protection. Their heads contain paired eyes and an obvious mouth with teeth.

Gills
Almost all fish have gills for breathing. The sharks and rays have paired gills in the throat, with openings to the outside known as gill slits. Bony fish have paired gills at the back of the head, with one opening covered by a flap of skin known as the operculum.

Swim bladder
Bony fish have a swim bladder containing air, and they are able to fill and empty it at will. In many bony fish the swim bladder controls buoyancy, allowing the fish to move up and down in the water.

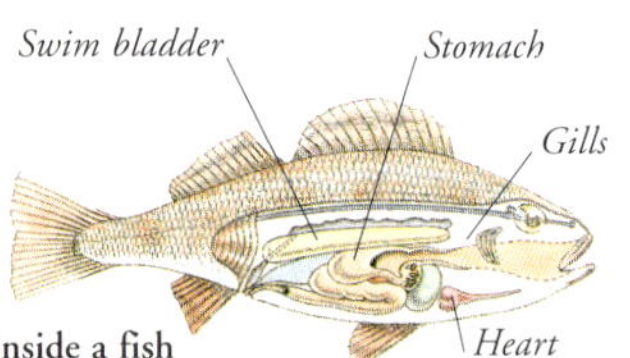

Swim bladder   *Stomach*

Gills

Inside a fish

Heart

Flatfish
Flatfish spend most of their lives lying on their sides, half buried and camouflaged in the sand on the seabed. Like most fish, the young develop in eggs. They hatch into normal larval fish that swim "the right way up" in the plankton.

10 days old

17 days old

35 days old

1 The larval fish has an eye on either side of its head.

2 One eye gradually "migrates" to the other side of the head.

3 An adult flatfish lies on one side. Its eyes are on top.

Fish groups
The fish are divided into three groups: jawless and primitive fish (cyclostomes), which include the lampreys and hagfish; cartilaginous fish (elasmobranchs), which include the sharks, rays, and ratfish; bony fish (teleosts), which include the more familiar fish, such as herring, cod, plaice, trout, eels, goldfish, sticklebacks, and guppies.

Caudal fin

Dorsal fin

Great white shark

Gill slits

Pectoral fin

Sharp teeth

Pike

Jawless fish
Hagfish and lampreys have funnel-shaped mouths. Lampreys attach themselves to other fish with their mouths and rasp away flesh with their teeth. Hagfish are scavengers.

Sea lamprey

Bony fish
These fish are divided into two groups – those with jointed bony fin rays, such as most fresh- and saltwater fish, and those with fleshy fin lobes, such as lungfish.

Cartilaginous fish
Sharks and rays have large mouths with many teeth in rows that are continually being replaced. Their skeletons are made of cartilage (gristle), instead of bones.

Where fish live
There are fish living wherever there is water. Some fish live in oceans, the largest numbers living in the shallow seas of the continental shelf. The most brightly coloured fish live on coral reefs. Other fish live on muddy, sandy, or rocky seashores, in estuaries, in rivers and streams, and even in temporary puddles.

On land
Inhabitants of Indo-Pacific mudflats and mangrove swamps, mudskippers are able to leave the water. They can stay on land for hours, absorbing oxygen through the mouth and pharynx. They have eyes on top of their heads for all-round vision.

Mudskipper

Red mullet

Rainbow trout

Oceans
The oceans provide a range of habitats for fish. Light-producing fish live in the deepest ocean trenches, while other fish live near hot volcanic vents. Some, such as sharks, roam the open oceans searching for smaller fish to eat.

Fresh water
Fish live in fast-flowing streams, slow-moving rivers, ponds, and lakes, and are suited to their habitat. Some have to be powerful swimmers or have suckers for holding on to stones. Others live in shoals or are camouflaged to avoid predators.

Protection

As well as scales, fish use colour, camouflage, or poisonous spines to protect themselves. The spiny puffer fish can take in water or air and swells up to more than twice its size. Some eels use an electric discharge, while other fish live in shoals, making it difficult for a predator to pick out any one individual.

Surgeon fish

Surgeon fish's blade folds in when not in use.

Cutting blade
The surgeon fish has a formidable cutting blade that lies in a groove. This defensive structure is a developed scale and is as sharp as a surgeon's scalpel. If attacked, the fish erects the blade and slices its opponent with a blow from its tail.

Cutting blade in a groove in the body

Blade extended

Clown fish

Plaice

Weever fish

Colour
Fish use colour to warn other fish that they are poisonous. Colour also helps some fish hide from predators. The fish's colour depends on its lifestyle. Cave fish have no colour; deep-sea fish are black; open-sea fish are a silvery colour.

Camouflage
Some fish look like the plants among which they live. The triple tail looks like a mangrove leaf, and the leafy sea-dragon and sargassum fish look like seaweed. The plaice can change colour to match the surrounding seabed.

Poison
Several fish are poisonous. The weever fishes are extremely dangerous. They lie partly buried and camouflaged in sand, waiting for food. The spines on their gill covers and dorsal fin can inject poison into anyone who steps on one.

Food

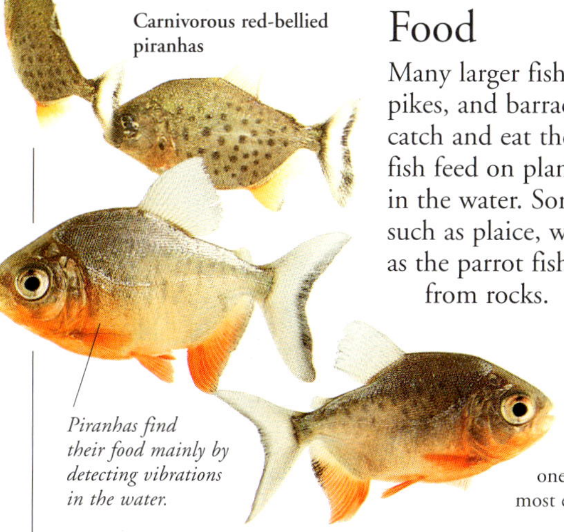

Carnivorous red-bellied piranhas

Piranhas find their food mainly by detecting vibrations in the water.

Many larger fish, including sharks, groupers, pikes, and barracudas, are predators and catch and eat their prey. Most smaller shoal fish feed on plankton, which floats around in the water. Some fish are bottom feeders, such as plaice, while others are grazers, such as the parrot fish, which rasps organisms from rocks.

Piranhas
These South American fish have strong jaws and sharp triangular teeth. A shoal of carnivorous piranhas can strip an animal to the bone in minutes. They are one of the most feared types of fish, but most eat mainly fruit and nuts.

Cleaner fish
Fish called cleaners, such as some wrasses, have "cleaning" stations where they wait for customers. The customers allow the cleaners to remove bits of food and parasites from their skin, gills, fins, and even right inside their mouths.

Angler fish with lure

Cleaner wrasse at work

Angler fish
Angler fish usually live in deep water. They have a dorsal fin ray modified into a fishing line, with a lure on the end to attract their prey. They can swallow fish much larger than themselves.

Reproduction

Most bony fish lay eggs in the water, and these are then fertilized by a male's sperm. The parents usually leave the eggs to their fate, but some species protect their young in their mouths, in pouches, or in nests. Some sharks, such as the dogfish, lay eggs in an egg case, while others bear live young.

Seahorses
Within 10 seconds of mating, the female seahorse transfers 200 fertilized eggs into the brood-pouch of the male. The male carries them around with him for four weeks until they are ready to hatch. The male then "gives birth", and the young seahorses swim away.

Stickleback eggs

Male stickleback's underside turns red in the breeding season.

Sticklebacks
Male sticklebacks make a nest and attract females by doing a zigzag dance. The female lays her eggs in the nest, and the male fertilizes them. He then protects the nest from any intruder until the young hatch and are ready to fend for themselves.

Male three-spined stickleback

Salmon
The Atlantic salmon lays its eggs in upland streams. The young, called parr, live there for three years; then they are called smolt. The smolt swim down-river to the sea and travel across the Atlantic. At maturity, the salmon return to spawn in the same stream where they hatched.

Adult salmon will leap up waterfalls on their journey upstream to spawn.

FIND OUT MORE CAMOUFLAGE AND COLOUR · LAKE AND RIVER WILDLIFE · MARSH AND SWAMP WILDLIFE · MIGRATION, ANIMAL · OCEAN WILDLIFE · POISONOUS ANIMALS · SHARKS AND RAYS

Fish

Marine

Blenny lives in shallow water and often rests on the bottom.

Royal gramma fish identifies itself to a mate with dazzling colours.

Zebra pipe fish hides in eel-grass.

Large black spots look like spots on a panther.

Cuckoo wrasse is a colourful fish that lives in British waters.

Red mullet is probably the most important commercial marine fish in the world.

Panther grouper is a lethal predator like its namesake.

Extremely poisonous fin ray spines

Both eyes are on the upper surface.

Plaice is a flat fish and can change colour to merge with the seabed.

Clown triggerfish has a spiny dorsal fin that it can lock erect like a trigger.

Juvenile lumpsucker

Lumpsucker has sucker-like fins for clinging safely to stones and rocks in rough seas.

Lionfish is brightly coloured, which warns its enemies that it is deadly poisonous.

Large free dorsal fin rays

Spiny boxfish has a rigid body from which it gets its name.

Port Jackson shark produces an egg case, or "mermaid's purse", in which the young develop.

John Dory sucks up its food in a tube formed by extendable jaws.

Butterfish is well camouflaged among the browny-green seaweed-covered rocks where it lives.

Angelfish are often brightly coloured.

Blue-ringed angelfish is flattened from side to side, making it difficult to see from the front.

Hatchetfish lives in the deep sea and has luminescent lights along its sides.

Large sensitive eyes for seeing in the dark

Freshwater

Bitterling lays its eggs in a freshwater mussel.

Large eyes for accurate shooting

Minnows live in shoals for protection.

Minnows are small silvery fish that live in clean, fast-flowing, freshwater streams.

Archerfish shoots a jet of water above the surface to capture its insect prey.

Uncoloured guppy, or toothcarp, bears its young alive, unlike most fish, which lay eggs.

Blue-ribbon eel is long and thin, allowing it to hide in narrow crevices.

Neon tetra is a very small, brightly coloured, tropical fish, often kept in aquaria.

FISHING INDUSTRY

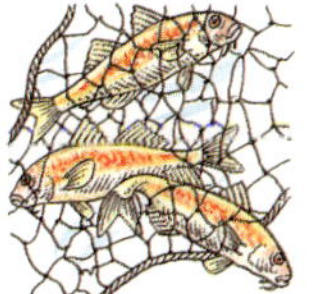

LONG BEFORE FARMING BEGAN, people fed themselves by hunting fish and land animals. Today, the fishing industry continues this hunting tradition. Fishing vessels go to sea from every country with a coastline. Small boats, such as the stern trawler, have few crew members, and fish within a day's sailing of their home port. The biggest fishing ships can stay at sea for months, and freeze their catch on board.

Fishing with lines
To catch valuable tuna, fishing boats trail a line as long as 180 km (112 miles, 97 nautical miles). Branching off this line are 200 smaller lines, each ending in a baited hook. This arrangement is known as a drifting longline.

Sea fishing

Most sea fish live within 50 m (165 ft) of the surface. They are concentrated in the shallow waters around the coasts of continents. In the past, the supply of sea fish appeared limitless. However, intensive fishing in areas that were once rich in fish, such as the Grand Banks of North America, has driven cod and other popular species to the edge of extinction.

Deep-water fishing
To catch demersal fish (those that live near the ocean floor), fishing boats sink bag-shaped nets in the water. The fish are trapped by towing the net along the bottom (trawling) or drawing the neck of the net closed (seine fishing). The boat then hauls in the net to land the catch.

Stern trawler

Fish-finding equipment in wheelhouse shows the crew where to find the biggest catch.

Deck winch drags the full net towards the boat.

Hoist lifts the net on to the boat.

Crew launch the trawl net over the boat's stern.

Seine fishing

Surface fishing

Net closes like a purse, entrapping fish.

Weighted net hangs down from floats.

Surface fishing
Many species of pelagic fish (those that live near the surface) swim together in large groups called shoals, and it is these shoals that fishing boats seek. They catch them by enclosing the shoal in a purse seine net, which is like a circular curtain. Pulling a line closes the bottom of the net, preventing the fish from escaping.

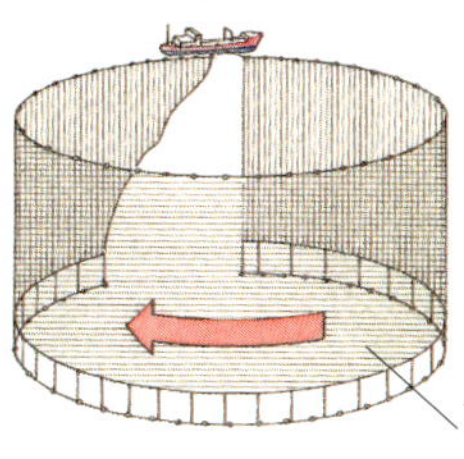

Ocean mammals
The oceans are also home to mammals. Fishing for whales, the world's largest mammals, has now almost ceased because their numbers fell so low. The fur of the seal makes it a target for hunters, and although few fishing vessels catch dolphins deliberately, many dolphins die because they become entangled in abandoned nets.

In the past, whaling crews made beautiful carvings out of the bones and teeth of sea mammals.

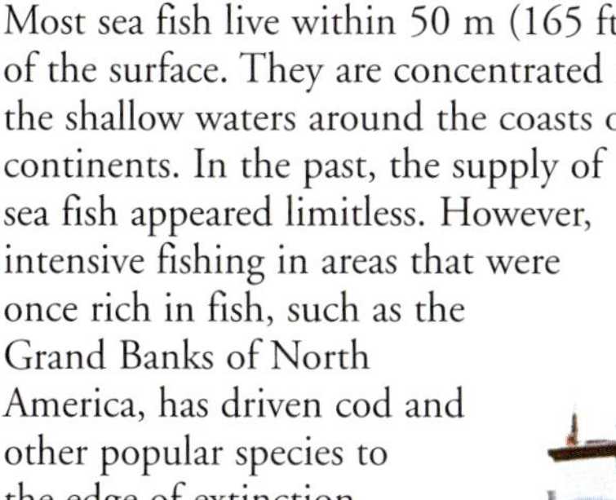

Traps
Bait lures lobsters into this basket-like "pot", which rests on the seabed in shallow water. Its funnel-shaped entrance makes escape impossible. Fish traps take many different forms: the Mediterranean tuna trap, for example, is like a maze of net corridors anchored to the seabed. There are even special aerial traps for catching flying fish.

Lobster pot

Freshwater fishing

Only 5 per cent of the world's fish catch comes from freshwater sources, such as rivers and lakes. However, in non-industrialized nations freshwater fishing with lines and nets is a vital industry, especially on great lakes such as those in East Africa's Rift Valley. In industrialized nations, anglers have to pay to fish on the few remaining stretches of unpolluted water.

Fur and feather make hook resemble an insect.

Freshwater rods

Barb

Point

Double hook | Treble hook | Fly-fishing bait | Weight

Fish farming
Just as farming produces meat more efficiently than hunting, farming fish is more efficient than catching them. Fish farms breed fish carefully to give good-quality stock, and protect the young fish in ponds or enclosures from predators. Carp and trout are the main freshwater farm fish.

Angling
Fishing for sport is known as angling, and is as ancient as fishing for food. Anglers fix a hook to a thin line and then cast it into the water using a long, flexible rod. To lure fish, anglers bait the hook with worms or insects. They may also use a "fly", which is a hook disguised as an insect.

FARMING FISH FOOD SHIPS AND BOATS SPORT WHALES AND DOLPHINS

FLAGS

FOR HUNDREDS of years, people have used flags as emblems, signals, or rallying points. Among the earliest flags were those flown in battle, so that soldiers could identify their leader and tell each side apart. The flag has since developed as a means of communication, used to send rapid signals, or as a symbol representing a nation or group. Every country has its own flag, as do many states and most political organizations.

Parts of a flag

A flag is usually made from brightly coloured fabric and is square or rectangular in shape – although more varied shapes, such as streamers, banners, and long, narrow pennons, were once popular. It is divided into four quarters (cantons): those near the pole are the hoist, and the others the fly. A special emblem often appears in the upper hoist canton.

Flying the flag
In Europe, flags are attached to the pole by passing the toggle through a loop (becket) in another rope (halyard). In the USA, flags have eyelets to which clips are attached. Inglefield clips have a quick-release mechanism, and are popular at sea. Parade flagstaffs are topped with decorative finials.

First flags

Many ancient armies carried standards, carved symbols on the end of a pole. The Roman standard first introduced cloth flags. These hung from horizontal poles, to make them easy to carry on horseback.

Homemade flag
The first flag was probably a piece of brightly coloured cloth tied to a stick. A plain red flag spelt danger to early peoples, just as it does today.

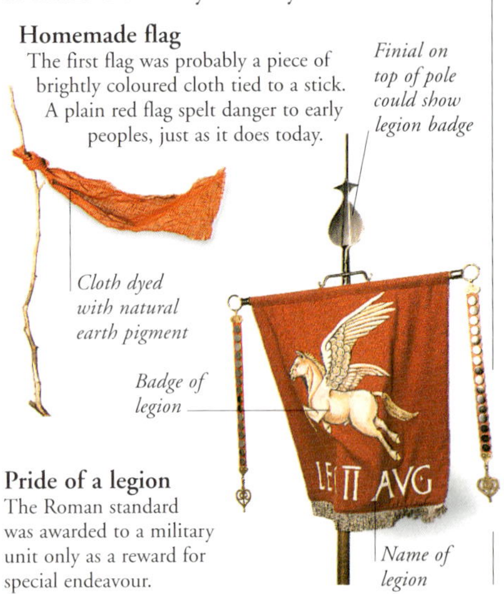

Pride of a legion
The Roman standard was awarded to a military unit only as a reward for special endeavour.

Uses of flags

Flags communicate across language barriers. At sea, the International Code of Signals is a system of signalling with flags: the meanings are the same in every language. In both sports and politics, flags also send messages that are understood universally.

The dove on the Greenpeace flag, a symbol of hope

Rallying cries
Modern flags may be developed to identify political movements, or for international medical or environmental groups. The emblems and colours represent the organization's ideals: for instance, a white background stands for peace, while olive branches symbolize reconciliation.

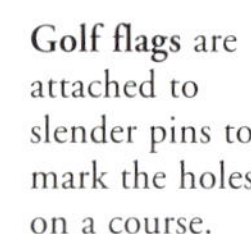

Soccer flags are raised to signal when the ball has gone out of play.

Golf flags are attached to slender pins to mark the holes on a course.

Sports flags
Flags are used in many sports for marking out the area of play or signalling to participants.

Plastic marker flags

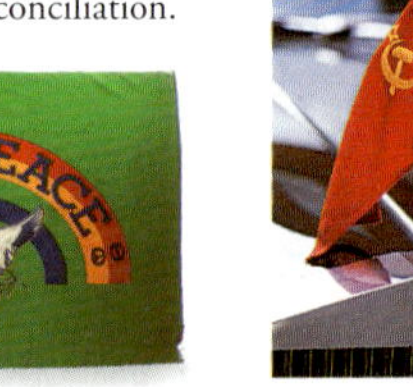

Political symbols
A symbol on a national flag can sum up political ideals that would otherwise take many words. The former Soviet red flag with its hammer and sickle symbol represented the workers and farmers who took part in the Russian Revolution.

Semaphore
This method of signalling with just two flags is still used at sea. Signallers can spell out a message quickly, simply by changing the position of their arms. Red and yellow flags are chosen because they can be seen over long distances.

FIND OUT MORE
FOOTBALL • PEACE MOVEMENTS • ROMAN EMPIRE • SHIPS AND BOATS • SIGNS AND SYMBOLS • SOVIET UNION • UNITED NATIONS

International Code of Signals

Alphabet and single flag messages

 **A** I have a diver down; keep well clear at slow speed.

 **B** I am taking in, or discharging, or carrying dangerous goods.

 **C** Yes.

 **D** Keep clear of me; I am manoeuvring with difficulty.

 **E** I am altering my course to starboard.

 **F** I am disabled; communicate with me.

 **G** I require a pilot (or, I am hauling nets).

 **H** I have a pilot on board.

 **I** I am altering my course to port.

 **J** I am on fire and have dangerous cargo on board; keep well clear of me.

 **K** I wish to communicate with you.

Two-flag messages

DX I am sinking.

 **L** You should stop your vessel instantly.

 **M** My vessel is stopped and making no way through the water.

 **N** No.

 **O** Man overboard.

 **P** All persons should report on board as vessel is about to proceed to sea.

NG You are in a dangerous position.

 **Q** My vessel is healthy and I require free pratique [permission to trade].

 **R** [No single letter meaning]

 **S** My engines are going astern.

 **T** Keep clear of me; I am engaged in pair trawling.

 **U** You are running into danger.

 **AC** I am abandoning my vessel.

 **V** I require assistance.

 **W** I require medical assistance.

 **X** Stop carrying out your intentions and watch my signals.

 **Y** I am dragging my anchor.

 **Z** I require a tug.

 **NH** You are clear of all dangers.

Numerals

FLIES

THEY MAY BE PESTS AT TIMES, but flies are remarkable insects. As their name suggests, they have mastered the power of flight. Fast and agile in the air, flies dart about, hover, and make lightning turns. There are about 90,000 different insects that we call flies. About 75,000 of these are true flies, which have only one pair of wings and belong to the insect group Diptera. The remainder form many other groups of insects with two pairs of wings. Unlike most other types of fly, the larvae of true flies are completely different from the adults. Often called maggots, they have simple bodies with no legs and are little more than eating machines.

Feeding

Fly larvae feed on foods such as microscopic organisms, living flesh, plants, and dung. The mouthparts of adult flies are adapted for a liquid diet. They have extendible tubes to draw fluids into their bodies. The feeding habits of flies cause many health problems worldwide, from stomach upsets to more serious illnesses such as cholera.

Tsetse fly

Abdomen swollen with blood

Bloodsuckers and predators
Bloodsuckers and flies that catch prey have piercing mouthparts that cut holes in their victims. They inject anti-clotting agents to keep blood flowing, or poison to kill the prey. Enzymes are also released to help break down the body contents.

Hoverfly

Nectar and waste feeders
Flies that feed on nectar or decaying matter have soft pads on the ends of their sucking mouthparts, that help soak up liquid food. On solid food, flies deposit saliva, then suck up the partly digested juice that results.

Features of a true fly

The body of an adult fly is clearly divided into three main parts: the head, thorax, and abdomen. The head bears the sucking mouthparts and a bulging pair of compound eyes, between which sprouts a pair of antennae. Attached to the thorax are the fly's six legs and its membranous wings. The abdomen contains most of the body organs.

Long hairs on thorax

Single pair of wings

Head

Antenna

Sponge-like mouthparts

Compound eye

Blue iridescence on abdomen

Sense hairs

The soles of the feet have taste buds on them.

Close-up of mouthparts

Mouthparts
The mouthparts of a blowfly end in soft spongy pads that enable them to suck up liquids.

Bluebottle feeding

Halteres of a crane fly

Flight stabilizers
True flies have a single pair of wings; the hindwings have developed into club-ended stubs called halteres. Halteres act as balancing organs that improve the fly's flight control and make it easier to change direction.

Breeding

After mating, female flies lay hundreds of eggs on a suitable feeding site for the larvae, that develop from the eggs. These sites may be in dung, soil, or water, or on leaves, dead bodies, or living animals. The larvae eat voraciously, and grow into pupae within which they change into their adult shape and form.

Robber flies mating

Bluebottle larvae

Mating
Before mating, flies may go through elaborate courtship rituals. Fruit flies dance on leaves, and gnats dance in the air. After mating, female robber flies commonly eat their mates.

Larvae
Fly eggs often hatch out into larvae on dead animals, which they begin to eat. The larvae, also called maggots, may live longer than the adult flies into which they develop.

Aquatic larvae

Mosquitos and many other bloodsucking flies lay their eggs in water. The larvae that develop float upside-down on the surface. They breathe through a tube attached to the abdomen, that pokes above the water. After pupation, the adult emerges to fly away.

Tube takes in air.

Mosquito larva

Types of fly

In addition to true flies, many other kinds of fly exist that all have two pairs of wings, such as dragonflies and mayflies. The young that emerge from their eggs have a more complicated body structure than the larvae of true flies – some even look like wingless versions of the adults.

Dragonflies
Dragonflies are large predators. They dart around in seach of other insects that they catch in flight with their long legs. They lay their eggs in water.

Giant compound eyes

Caddis flies
Adult caddis flies always live near water. Their larvae live underwater, and carry with them a protective case made of plant debris or sand.

Long antenna

Mayflies
Young mayflies live below water. After growing wings, they leave the water and form swarms in the air. The adults mate, lay their eggs, then die a few hours later.

Long, thin legs

Lacewings
Lacewings often hibernate in houses over winter. The adults and larvae prey on other insects such as aphids. They are weak fliers.

Delicate wings

ARTHROPODS   DISEASES   EGGS   FLIGHT, ANIMAL   INSECTS   MARSH AND SWAMP WILDLIFE

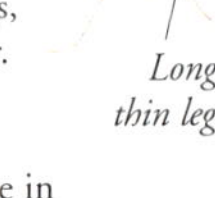

FLIGHT, ANIMAL

THE ONLY ANIMALS CAPABLE of powered flight are birds, bats, and insects. Some other animals can glide for short distances. Flight is very useful. It helps the animals to find food, escape from predators, and migrate long distances. Flying animals need wings, powerful wing muscles, a streamlined shape, and a lightweight body. They also need to eat lots of food to give them the energy to flap their wings.

Insects

A small insect, such as a mosquito, flaps its wings 1,000 times a second. Most insects flap about 520 times a second. Dragonflies are the fastest insect fliers, reaching nearly 300 kmh (190 mph). Some insects, such as flies, have one pair of wings. Others, such as bees, have two pairs.

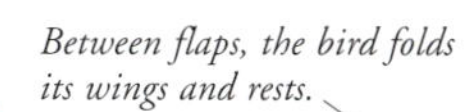

Vertical muscle contracts, moving the wings up

Horizontal muscle contracts, moving the wings down.

Wing muscles
Insect wings developed from their hard body covering. They are not modified legs, like the wings of birds or bats. Insects do not have any muscles on the wings. Instead, their wing muscles are inside the thorax, the middle part of the body.

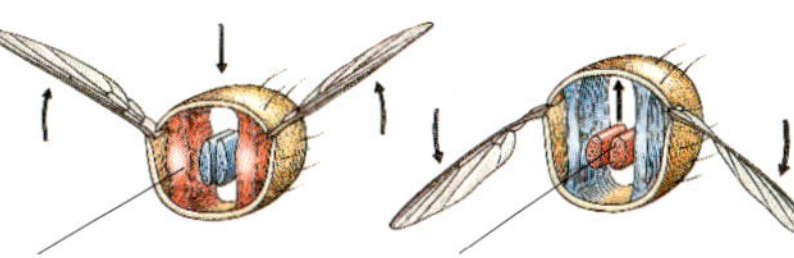

Cockchafer take-off
The cockchafer is a beetle with two pairs of wings. The front wings are hard wing cases, which are held out of the way during flight. They give the beetle some lift when it flies fast. The flexible back wings flap up and down to provide the power for flight.

Minla in flight

Birds

A bird's wings are an aerofoil shape – curved on top and slightly hollow underneath. As the wings move through the air, a difference in air pressure is created above and below, which lifts the bird up into the air. A bird steers by changing the angle of one or both wings, twisting its wings, and spreading and twisting its tail.

Between flaps, the bird folds its wings and rests.

Tail used to steer and change direction

Red-tailed minlas have an up-and-down flight.

Forward flight
Most small birds, such as this minla of eastern Asia, fly by flapping their wings up and down. As the wings go down, they push air backwards, moving the bird forwards. As the wings go up, the feathers at the wingtips move apart to allow air to slip through.

Feathers closed for the downstroke

Gliding albatross

Gliding
Some large birds rarely flap their wings. Albatrosses and other large seabirds glide on strong winds rising off the waves. Albatrosses can travel for hundreds of kilometres a day. Large land birds, such as vultures and eagles, float on columns of rising hot air called thermals.

Hovering
Hummingbirds are among the birds that hover. They beat their wings in a figure-of-eight pattern, producing lift on both the upstroke and downstroke. They can also fly sideways, straight up and down, backwards, and even upside-down.

Swan taking off

Taking off
Small birds take off by jumping into the air and flapping their wings. They may take off straight from the ground or from a perch. A large, heavy bird, such as a swan, cannot do this. It needs to run along while flapping its wings to create enough lift for take-off.

Bats

The only mammals able to fly, bats are more acrobatic than birds. They have four large pairs of flight muscles and several smaller pairs, while birds have only two pairs. Each wing consists of skin stretched between four long fingers.

Wing is made of an elastic membrane covered with skin.

The bat flexes its arm bones up and down to flap its wings.

Long narrow wings are for fast flight in open areas.

Horseshoe bats find prey by echolocation.

Thumbs are used for clinging to surfaces.

Gliding animals

Some animals can glide slowly downwards. They have developed large fins, or webs or flaps of skin, which they spread out to slow their fall. They have to be able to judge speeds and distances accurately.

Flying squirrel

Flying squirrel
Flaps of skin allow a flying squirrel to glide up to 100 m (330 ft) between trees. The squirrel uses its tail as a rudder, and has sharp claws to grasp the surface on landing.

Flying fish
To escape predators, flying fish swim fast along the surface, then take off and glide for up to 50 m (160 ft), with their huge fins held out.

Flying gecko
The gecko (above) has flaps of skin along the sides of its body and tail. It spreads out the flaps to glide between trees. It has webbed feet to help with steering.

Flying fish

F

FLIGHT, HISTORY OF

EVERY DAY, MILLIONS OF PEOPLE fly to destinations all over the world. Planes are a common sight in the skies, but, despite their widespread use, they were first developed only about 90 years ago. The urge to fly is ancient, but by the start of the 20th century, the only flying machines were hot-air balloons, airships, and gliders. World War I stimulated the development of aeroplanes and, by the end of World War II, advances had resulted in jets and rockets. Since then, flight technology has produced supersonic planes and space travel.

Flying machine designed by Leonardo da Vinci in the 15th century

Copying the birds

Wings are the part of an aircraft that provide the upwards lift needed to keep it in the air. Successful aeroplanes were impossible to build before people understood how wings worked. Early attempts at flight concentrated on copying the flapping action of birds, which proved to be impractical because a human's muscles are far too weak. Many "bird men" were killed trying to fly.

First controlled flight

The first controlled flight of a powered aeroplane took place on 17 December 1903 in Kitty Hawk, North Carolina, USA. The plane, *Flyer I*, flew 36 m (119 ft) in a flight that lasted under 12 seconds: it is nonetheless perhaps the most famous flight of all time. *Flyer I* was designed and built by the Wright brothers, Orville and Wilbur, after years of experiments with kites and gliders. It was powered by a petrol engine they built themselves.

Flyer I climbed to a height of 3 m (10 ft).

Wilbur Wright watches his brother Orville take off.

Warplanes

The military's interest in the potential of aeroplanes as weaponry was central to the advancement of flight technology. During World War I (1914–18), warplanes were transformed from being slow and vulnerable to being fast, easily manoeuvrable fighting machines. Huge bomber and fighter planes were made in this period.

Protective clothing worn by World War I pilots included flying helmet, goggles and gauntlets.

Airships

Airships are held aloft by a vast gas-filled envelope and driven forward by engines with propellers. Airships were an important form of passenger and military transport until long-distance aircraft were developed in the 1940s.

Amelia Earhart

American aviation pioneer Amelia Earhart (1898–1937) set several long-distance flight records. She was the first woman to fly solo across the Atlantic. In 1937, in a bid to fly round the world, she disappeared near New Guinea.

Modern age

The basis for the modern aeroplane first appeared in the 1920s. It was a monoplane (single-winged) aircraft. The wing was made of metal, as was the fuselage. All aircraft had piston engines and propellers until the late 1930s, when a new type of engine, the jet, was invented.

Harrier GR5 jet fighter

Jets

A turbojet engine allows aircraft to fly much faster and more quietly than a propeller engine. Jet aircraft were increasingly used after World War II and became standard for fighter aircraft and for long-distance passenger planes.

Ariane launch vehicle

Biplane of 1917

Biplane

World War I pilots flew biplane (twin-winged) fighters. Built from wood and fabric, biplanes were sturdier than monoplanes, but flying them was little fun. The cockpit was open to the cold and wet, and to spits of oil from the engine. Larger fighters had a second cockpit for a navigator and gunner. Single-seaters had a machine gun that fired through the spinning propeller.

Boarding pass

Airline ticket

Passenger flight

Fast, comfortable, and affordable air travel had become accessible by the 1960s. Today, millions of passengers fly around the world in the Boeing 747, a so-called "jumbo jet" which has quiet, turbofan engines.

Space flight

The first rockets powerful enough to reach space were built in the late 1950s. Today, modern launch vehicles and re-usable spacecraft, such as the Shuttle, make going into orbit almost an everyday event.

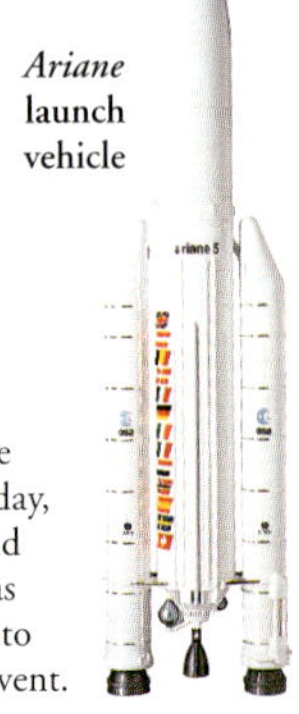

FLIGHTLESS BIRDS

FLYING IS A VERY USEFUL WAY of moving, but it does have drawbacks. It uses a lot of energy, and it is possible only for animals with a light body. During the course of evolution, some birds have given up flight and the problems it brings. Instead, they run, or, as is the case with penguins, they swim; some can move extremely fast. There are about 40 species of flightless birds alive today, including kiwis, emus, and the world's biggest bird, the ostrich. Many more flightless species, including some record-breaking giants, existed in the past, and some of today's species are also in danger of extinction.

Long neck with sparse feathers

Weak, fanlike wings used in courtship rituals.

Females are slightly smaller than males, with brown plumage instead of black.

Two large clawed toes on each foot

Kiwis

These medium-sized birds are found only in the forests of New Zealand. Their wings are only about 5 cm (2 in) long, and their body is covered with a unique plumage that looks like hair. Kiwis are nocturnal and because they have poor eyesight, they find food mainly by smelling it.

Ostrich

The ostrich is the world's largest bird. It can run at up to 65 kmh (40 mph), and uses its speed and stamina to outdistance most of its enemies. An ostrich's feet have two toes, and each toe ends in a large claw. If an ostrich is cornered, it uses these claws as deadly weapons to defend itself.

Ostrich crèche
Young ostriches are guarded by an adult male. Several families of chicks gather together, forming a group called a crèche.

Hatching
The shell of an ostrich egg is thicker than a china mug, but not as hard. The young ostrich breaks out by kicking and pecking at the shell.

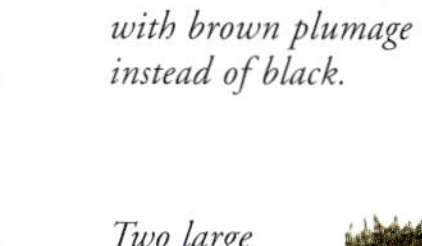

1 The chick turns its body as it pecks and pushes at the shell.

2 Half the shell is in pieces, and the chick is almost free of the egg.

3 The chick tumbles out and will soon start to look for food.

Sensory, whisker-like feathers at the base of the beak

Small wings are hidden under the body plumage.

Hard "helmet," or casque

Rheas escape from danger by running away.

Cassowaries
These large, flightless birds live in dense forests in northern Australia and New Guinea. They use their claws as weapons and have been known to kill people.

Rheas
There are two species of rheas, both of which live on the open plains in South America. Young rheas have bright stripes, but the adults are grayish-brown.

Strong legs with large feet

This egg is shown in proportion to the kiwi above.

Probing beak
The kiwi has nostrils at the tip of its long, curved beak, instead of near its head. It uses its beak to find food on the forest floor.

Kiwi egg
The kiwi's egg is 13 cm (5 in) long, and is a quarter of the female's weight. Relative to her body, the female kiwi lays the largest eggs of all birds.

Emus
Found only in Australia, emus are the second largest birds in the world, after the ostrich. Emus live in large flocks and wander long distances in search of food. They can cause problems on farms by raiding crops.

OSTRICH

SCIENTIFIC NAME *Struthio camelus*

ORDER Struthioniformes

FAMILY Struthionidae

DISTRIBUTION Tropical western and eastern Africa, and southern Africa

HABITAT Savannah and semi-desert

DIET Fruit, seeds, leaves, small animals

SIZE Height up to 2.4 m (8 ft); weight up to 154 kg (340 lb)

LIFESPAN About 30 years

FIND OUT MORE AUSTRALIAN WILDLIFE · BIRDS · EGGS · FLIGHT, ANIMAL · GRASSLAND WILDLIFE · PENGUINS · SOUTH AMERCIAN WILDLIFE

FLOWERS

THE FIRST flowering plants appeared about 120 million years ago. They are now the largest group of plants, and are widespread. Flowers are the advanced reproductive structures of plants. The majority of them are pollinated by the wind or by animals. Over millions of years, flowers and insects have co-evolved to produce some very complex and interesting relationships.

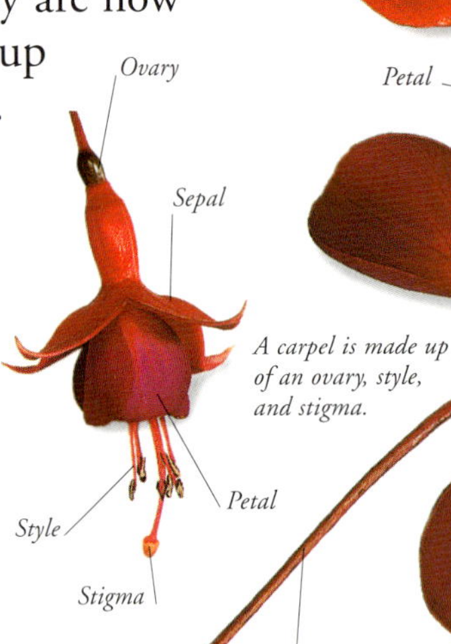

Fuchsia flower

Ovary
Sepal
Style
Petal
Stigma

Sepal

Petal

Ovary

A carpel is made up of an ovary, style, and stigma.

Anther

Filament

A stamen is made up of an anther and a filament.

Stigma

Style

Anthers produce pollen grains.

When the anthers are ripe, they split to release masses of pollen.

Petals are brightly coloured to attract insects.

Flower stalk

The flower is the structure that brings about sexual reproduction in the plant.

Sepal

Sepals enclose the flower when in bud.

Parts of a flower

A plant's reproduction organs are inside the flowers. Stamens are male and produce pollen. The female organs are called carpels. These contain ovules, which develop into seeds. A ring of petals attracts pollinators, and sepals protect the flower when in bud.

Pollination

In order for seeds to develop, a flower has to be pollinated. Pollen from the stamens of a flower of the same species must stick to the plant's stigma. Cross-pollination occurs when pollen from one plant lands on the flowers of another. If a flower is pollinated by its own pollen, it is called self-pollination.

Bee at a *Narcissus* flower

Insect pollination
Flowers are mostly pollinated by insects. These are attracted to the flowers by their petals, a scent, and a supply of nectar or pollen to eat. The pollen sticks to a visiting insect and is carried to another flower.

Freesia

Tobacco plant

Scent and colour
The colour and scent of a flower attract insects or other animals. Drops of sugary nectar secreted at the base of the petals provide food for the insects, which are dusted with pollen while they drink. Flowers are often sweetly scented, but some smell unpleasant, especially those pollinated by flies.

Wattle

Water pollination
Aquatic plants may have aerial, submerged, or floating flowers. A few use the surface film of water to carry pollen. The flowers float in shallow dips. The pollen slides into these and pollinates the flowers.

Starwort

Wind pollination
Some plants rely on wind to waft their pollen from one flower to another. Their flowers may have no petals, or just tiny ones. They are often arranged in catkins with conspicuous stamens and stigmas.

Hazel catkins and pollen

Bird pollination
Many flowers that rely on birds to pollinate them are red or orange – colours that attract birds. The flowers tend to be tubular so that birds can dip their beaks in. Stamens dust the birds' heads with sticky pollen.

Hummingbird at a thistle flower

Mammal pollination
Important mammal pollinators include some species of tropical bat and many types of tiny Australian possum. They pollinate flowers as they feed on nectar and pollen.

Pygmy possum feeding on a *Banksia* flower

Insect mimics

Many orchids have such specialized partnerships that only one type of insect serves as a pollinator. Some orchids look and smell so like a female insect, that males of that species try to mate with them, picking up pollen as they do so.

Bee orchid

An orchid's pollen is produced in small clumps called pollinia.

The bee orchid can be pollinated by a bee, but is often self-pollinated by the wind.

Part of the flower looks and smells just like a bee.

Flowers
Insect-pollinated

Bramble pollinators include beetles and bees.

Bell heather is pollinated by short-tongued bees.

Primrose flowers appear in the spring.

Hollow-stemmed asphodel has hollow stems and leaves.

Red clover has a head of tubular flowers.

Greater periwinkle is pollinated by bees.

Mirror orchid has pollen in clumps called pollinia.

Anemone pavonina is pollinated by insects.

Magnolia flowers have thick, waxy petals.

Corn marigold flowerhead has many tiny flowers.

Fox and cubs has strap-shaped ray florets.

Bastard balm attracts bees with its large petal.

Dwarf elder has small flowers clustered together.

Early dog violet has dark veins, which guide insects.

Wild pansy is pollinated by long-tongued bees.

Foxglove is pollinated by bumblebees.

Thorow-wax has clusters of flowers called umbels.

Marsh cinquefoil has much larger sepals than petals.

Red valerian has tiny tubular flowers pollinated by moths and butterflies.

Carline thistle has yellow flowers surrounded by stiff, spiny bracts.

Honeysuckle has scented flowers which attract honeybees and hawk moths.

Cornflower has scented flowers and is pollinated by flies and bees.

Common rockrose is pollinated by insects, but can be self-pollinating.

Red campion is pollinated by long-tongued bees and also by hoverflies.

Bird- and mammal-pollinated

Fuchsia is pollinated mostly by birds.

Passionflower is pollinated by nectar-drinking birds.

Silver wattle flowers attract birds and possums.

Nasturtium flowers are pollinated by birds.

Hibiscus dusts hawk moths and birds with pollen.

Urn plant flowers are surrounded by spiny bracts.

Wind-pollinated

Broad-leaved pondweed has a dense spike of flowers.

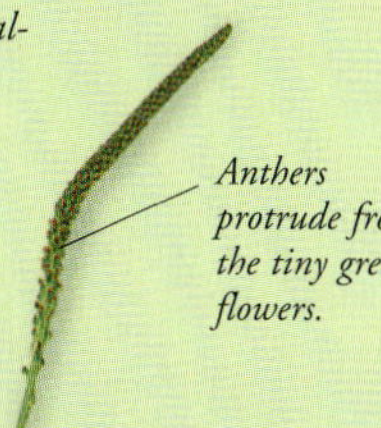

Greater plantain has purple anthers.

Armenian oak has male flowers in yellow catkins.

Sand couch has flowers in stalkless spikelets.

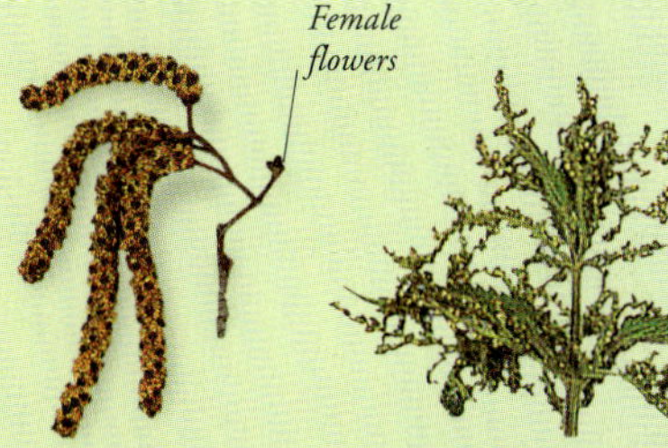

Alder has male flowers in long, dangling catkins.

Stinging nettle has catkins of male or female flowers.

FOOD

WE ARE WHAT WE EAT: our bodies get the energy and nourishment they need from our daily diet. Not having enough of the right food, or eating too much of the wrong food, causes ill-health. Food and eating are important in other ways too. Many countries have a distinctive cuisine (cooking style), which reflects the eating habits of its people and the ingredients available locally. In many industrialized nations, cooking is a hobby as well as a necessary task. Today there is concern about levels of chemicals in food, and many people choose an organic diet.

Processing and preserving

Even before they are cooked, most foods must be processed to make them ready for cooking: for example, wheat must be ground into flour before it can be baked as bread. Preserving food allows it to be stored for use later; this reduces the risk of shortages, and prolongs availability. A food industry has grown up to provide the food we eat, and process, preserve, and package it.

Preparing cassava

Cassava
Many foods are indigestible without processing but bitter cassava, the main food in many tropical areas, is actually poisonous. Grating, pressing, and heating the root removes the deadly cyanide it contains.

Food preservation: freezing peas

Viner

Frozen peas

1 Until frozen peas were invented, the only peas most people could eat were dried or tinned. A machine called a viner harvests the peas when they are sweet enough to be frozen. It tumbles them in a drum to remove the pods. These are ploughed back into the field as fertilizer.

2 Once at the factory, the peas are washed and blanched. They are then carried on a conveyor to the freezing chamber. On the way, jets of cold air prevent them sticking together. In the chamber, the peas are blast-frozen at a temperature of -18°C (-2°F).

3 Before packaging, the peas are assessed for quality and taste. Fresh vegetables begin to lose their nutrients as soon as they are picked. Because these peas have been frozen within two and a half hours, they are fresher than fresh peas in a shop.

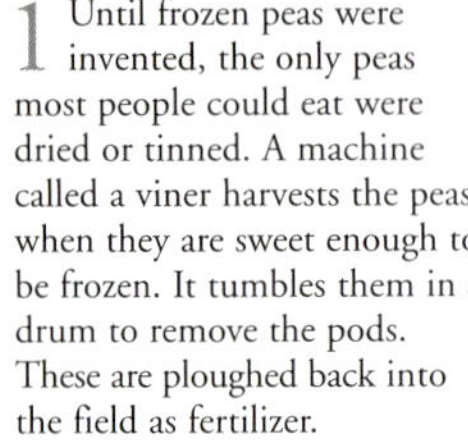
Cocoa beans

Chocolate
Chocolate is a food product derived from the cocoa bean. The Aztecs of Mexico enjoyed a chocolate drink, flavoured with chilli. When the Spanish conquered Mexico in the 16th century, they introduced the drink to Europe. People began to eat solid chocolate from about 1630, but chocolate bars were a luxury until the 20th century.

Frozen food
Freezing food to preserve it dates from prehistoric times in cold regions. Following the appearance of home electric refrigerators in 1913, frozen vegetables first went on sale in the USA in 1930.

Peas in the pod

Frozen vegetables

Fast food is food that is mass-prepared and served quickly in takeaway outlets. The hamburger is a popular fast food in many western countries.

A delicacy in France

Popular in Japan

Made with pig's blood

Jews and Muslims do not eat pork.

Frog's legs   **Seaweed**   **Black pudding**   **Snails**   **Pork sausages**

What is food?

Anything humans can digest counts as food. Worldwide, diets vary widely: food habits are influenced by availability, climate, and religious, moral, or social factors. Ideally, a daily diet should include staple, energy-giving carbohydrates, such as rice or pasta, plus proteins, fats, vitamins, and minerals. In reality, poverty or warfare make this impossible in many places.

Preparing food

Although some foods, such as salad vegetables and fruit, are delicious when raw, many foods need to be cooked first. Cooking makes food tastier and easier to digest. Cooking root vegetables, for instance, makes their starch grains absorb water, swell, and burst, releasing essential nutrients.

Salad

Fennel

Orange

Steaming fish is a healthy way to cook it.

Cooking methods
There are many cooking methods, such as simmering food in water, which heats it to just under 100°C (212°F). Only a few foods, such as eggs, cook at temperatures lower than this. Grilling or frying in oil heats food to a much higher temperature, cooking it faster.

Hunger and famine

Each year, 800 million people cannot get enough food to lead healthy lives, despite food surpluses in other parts of the world. Children suffer most. Malnutrition in children severely damages their physical and mental development. Every year in the developing world, famine (widespread starvation) occurs when insects, plant diseases, drought, or warfare destroy crops, and a harvest fails.

FIND OUT MORE   DIGESTION   FARMING   HEALTH AND FITNESS   TRADE AND INDUSTRY

Food

Types of food

Rice is a staple food for Southern
Asia and parts of Africa.

Wheat is a staple in North America,
Europe, Australia, and parts of Asia.

Maize (corn) is a staple food in some
African, Asian, and American countries.

Starchy roots are a good
source of carbohydrate.

Vegetables are an important
source of vitamins.

Pulses (beans and peas)
are rich in protein.

Nuts and seeds can be
pressed to make oils.

Fruits are an important
source of vitamins.

Sugars and honey
sweeten food.

Meat is a major
protein source.

Fish and shellfish are a
low-fat protein source.

Eggs are a valuable
source of protein.

Milk and milk products provide
protein and important minerals.

Fats and oils
store energy.

Spices and herbs add
flavour to a meal.

World cookery

Australia: meats grilled out-
of-doors on a barbecue

India: vegetable curry
and *roti* (wheat bread)

Spain: *paella,* rice simmered with
chicken, seafood, and spices

France: *bouillabaisse,* fish
soup, served with bread

Mexico: *buritto,* a pancake
with chilli, meat, beans

Vietnam: spring rolls filled
with pork, prawns, noodles

Morocco: chicken
baked with spices

United States: pork ribs
with black-eyed peas

China: roast duck with
an aromatic seasoning

Italy: *fettucini,* a kind of
pasta, in a tomato sauce

Thailand: *pad thai,*
Thai fried noodles

Japan: *sushi,* extremely fresh,
raw fish, with rice and seaweed

United Kingdom: roast beef,
gravy, and roast potatoes

Russia: *borscht* (beetroot
soup) with *blinis* (pancakes)

FOOD WEBS AND CHAINS

THE LIVES OF DIFFERENT species in a wildlife community are linked together through the process of feeding. As plants and animals grow and are eaten by others, energy and food substances locked up in their body tissues pass on along a chain. These food chains interlink with one another, and the resulting network is called a food web. The number of different animals and plants in a community is naturally balanced. If the balance is upset it can affect the whole web.

Food webs

In a simple food chain, a plant is eaten by a herbivore (a plant-eating animal), that in turn is eaten by a carnivore (a meat-eating animal). In nature, food chains are usually longer than this, and they connect with other chains to form a web. The arrows in this diagram show how different plant foods on a typical African savannah are eaten by a range of animals, that, in turn, provide food for various other animals.

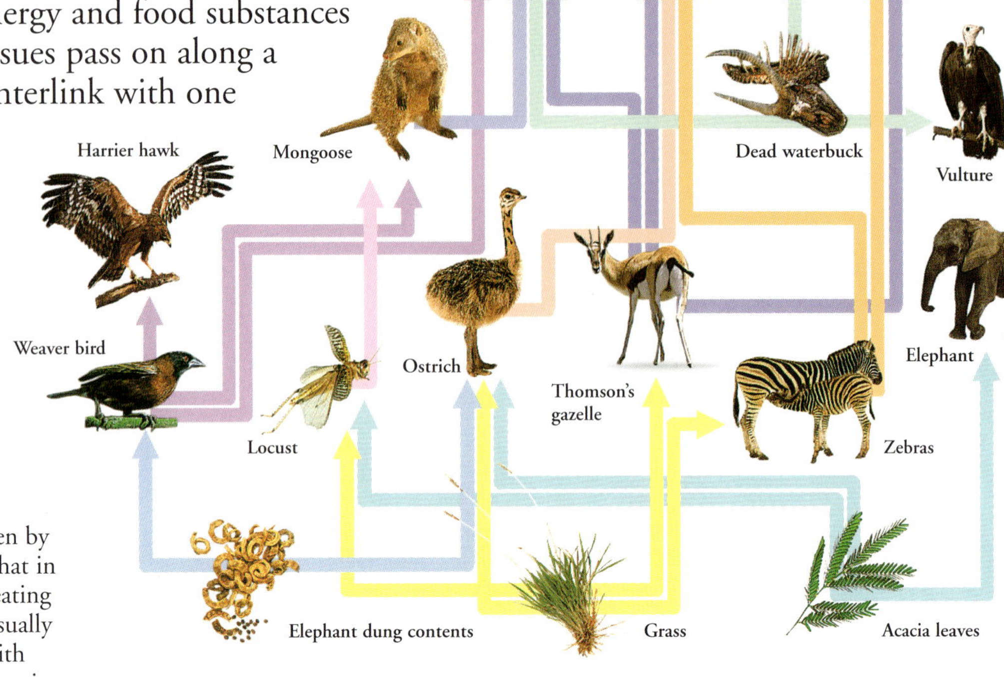

Decomposers
Some animals, fungi, and bacteria feed on dead or waste plant and animal tissue. They turn it back into simple substances, which plants use to grow.

Producers
In ecology, plants are called producers. They start the food chain by using the sun's energy to produce food from simple substances.

Consumers
Animals are known as consumers because they get the biological material they need for life from the plants or other animals that they eat or consume.

Top predator

The tawny owl at the top of this food chain is known as the top predator. An owl needs to eat many weasels and rodents to meet its energy needs.

The number of animals or plants represents the amount of energy available to the next level.

Trophic pyramids

Ecologists call each stage in a food chain a trophic level. These levels can be represented as a pyramid. Animals use much of the energy they gain from their food to grow. They also use energy to live, to move about, breed, feed, and avoid their enemies. This means that at each trophic level there is less energy available to the next level.

Secondary consumers

Weasels are secondary consumers because they get energy from the plants through other consumers. There are more weasels in a community than the owls that hunt them.

Primary consumers

Mice and voles get energy directly from plants. They use a lot of energy; many are needed to support the weasels.

Primary producers

Energy is stored in plants. It takes a large quantity to support the rodents.

Population cycles

A change in the population of one species affects the population of other species in the food chain. The lemming population in the tundra and Arctic rises and falls on roughly a four-year cycle. When there are lots of lemmings, Arctic foxes, which hunt them, breed more successfully, so their numbers increase too.

Arctic fox

Giant African land snail

Partula snail

Upsetting the balance

When the giant African land snail was taken to Pacific islands, the snails destroyed vegetation because there was nothing to prey on them. Another type of snail was released to eat their eggs, but these began to wipe out the native *Partula* snail instead.

FOOTBALL

THE VARIOUS FORMS OF FOOTBALL are among the most popular sports to play and watch. Association football, or soccer, is played in almost every country by men and women. Rugby games are less widespread, but the new professional rugby union is becoming increasingly international. American football, although watched worldwide on television, is played little outside the United States. Other "national" games include Australian football, played chiefly in the state of Victoria, and Gaelic football, an Irish game.

Soccer ball

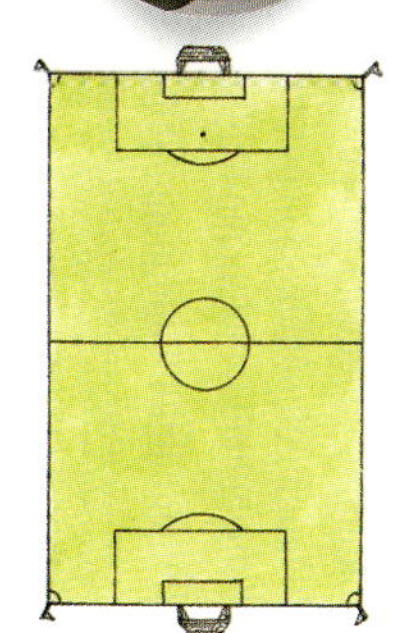
Soccer pitch

Soccer

Soccer is a kicking game played 11-a-side. The goalkeeper is the only person allowed to handle the ball. The object is to propel the ball into the opposition's goal with a foot or the head. A game lasts 90 minutes, with a 15-minute interval plus, in some knock-out competitions, an extra 15 minutes each way.

Helmet

Face mask made from unbreakable plastic coated in rubber

Shoulder pads

Upper arm pad

Rib pads tie to shoulder pads.

Hip pad

Breeches

Thigh pad

American football

A handling game, American football is played 11-a-side with limitless substitution from 40 players or more. It is divided into short bursts of action as the attacking team advances in a series of "downs". Points are awarded chiefly for touchdowns and field goals.

American football

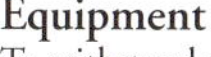
American football field

Equipment

To withstand the crunching tackles and blocks, players wear extensive protective padding under their uniform, the amount and type depending on their role. Players wear a number from 1 to 99 to identify them.

World Cup

The soccer World Cup is as popular as the Olympics. About 170 countries enter competitions to qualify for the 32 places in the finals, which take place every four years.

Pelé

Brazilian soccer star Pelé (b. 1940) won universal acclaim when he inspired Brazil to win the World Cup for the first time in 1958. His performances in Brazil's 1970 triumph have gone down in soccer folklore. In a first-class career he scored 1,281 goals.

Women's soccer

In 1991, the first women's soccer World Cup was held, and women's soccer was accepted as an Olympic sport in 1996. In many countries, girls now begin playing soccer at school.

Australian football

Australian football is played 18-a-side on a huge oval field. Players kick, catch, and run with the ball which must be grounded every 10 m (33 ft). A goal, kicked between the inner posts, is worth six points; a behind, kicked inside the outer posts, scores one point.

Rugby

The rugby codes are rugby union and rugby league. They are handling games featuring running, hand-to-hand passing, tackling, and kicking. Points are scored for a try – touching the ball down over the opposition goal line, or a goal – kicking the ball over the cross bar and between the posts. The two codes have a slightly different ball and pitch.

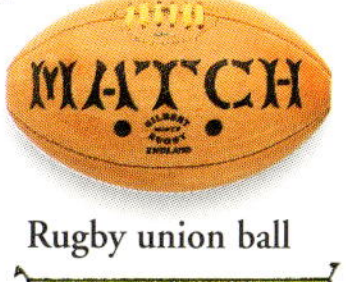
Rugby union ball

Rugby union pitch

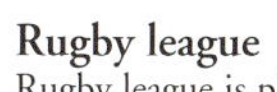

Rugby union

This is played 15-a-side with eight forwards, two halfbacks, four three-quarters, and one full-back. It features scrums (shown here), line-outs to restart play, and tactical kicking. Tries score five points and conversions two points.

Rugby league

Rugby league is played 13-a-side. A tackled player may rise and play the ball with his foot. After six successive tackles, a team must give up the ball to the other team. Tries score four points, goals one or two.

Gaelic football

This is played 15-a-side with a round ball. It is a cross between soccer and Australian football. The ball may be kicked, fisted, and passed hand-to-hand. Points are scored by kicking the ball between the posts, under the bar for three points, over for one point.

FIND OUT MORE

BALL GAMES

OLYMPIC GAMES

SPORT

TENNIS AND OTHER RACKET SPORTS

FORCE AND MOTION

THE WORLD IS NEVER STILL — traffic and pedestrians rush along busy streets, clouds race across the sky, and the Earth turns on its axis and whirls around the Sun. Forces make all this motion, or movement, possible. A force is a push or a pull that causes an object to start or stop moving, or to change its speed or direction. When forces combine, they can hold things still or make things balance. The study of the way objects move when forces act upon them is called dynamics.

Speed and acceleration

An object's speed is how far it moves in a period of time. Speed in a particular direction is called velocity. Acceleration is the rate at which an object's velocity changes.

A sprinter who runs 60 metres in 12 seconds has an average speed of 5 m/s.

The sprinter's feet push against the starting blocks.

The force exerted by the sprinter's feet propels him forward.

A sprinter's acceleration is greatest during the first few seconds of a race.

Combining forces

Equal forces acting on an object in opposite directions will have no effect. If the forces are not equal, or if they do not act in opposite directions, they will combine to give an overall force called the resultant.

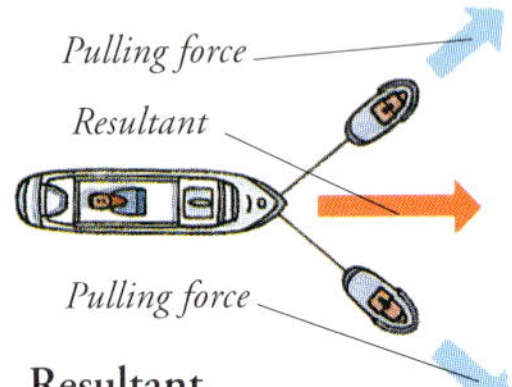

Pulling force

Resultant

Pulling force

Resultant

Two tugboats helping an ocean liner into port do not pull in the direction the ship needs to travel. They pull at an angle to each other so that the resultant force moves the ship straight ahead.

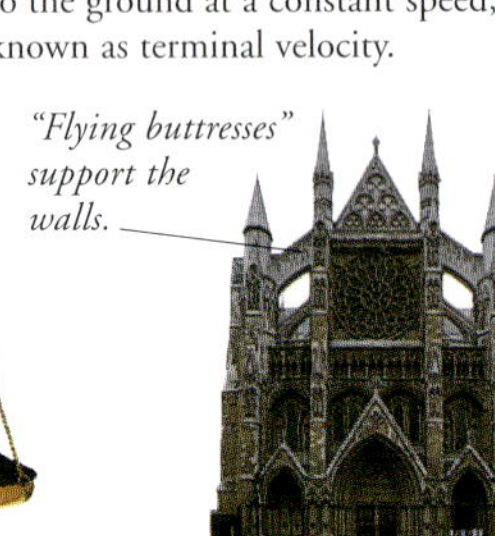

Equilibrium

An object is in equilibrium when the forces acting upon it balance. This set of scales is in equilibrium when two equal masses are placed on the pans, because gravity pulls on each pan with the same force.

Equal masses

Terminal velocity

Gravity pulls a parachute downwards, but air resistance pushes upwards with an equal force. There is no resultant, because the forces cancel each other out. The parachute cannot accelerate, so it falls to the ground at a constant speed, known as terminal velocity.

"Flying buttresses" support the walls.

Statics

Statics is the study of forces acting on stationary objects in equilibrium. It is important in building design, because a building will collapse if the forces acting upon it do not balance.

Inertia

An object's mass makes it resist a force that tries to change its state of motion, whether it is moving or at rest. This resistance is called inertia. The greater an object's mass, the more inertia it has. For example, the same force will accelerate a small car more than a loaded truck, because the car has a smaller mass and less inertia.

Momentum

When a moving object collides with a stationary one, the result depends upon a quantity called momentum. An object's momentum is calculated by multiplying its mass by its velocity. For example, a heavy bowling ball has more momentum than a light plastic ball moving at the same velocity, because it has a greater mass.

The mass of the bowling ball gives it enough momentum to scatter the pins.

The lighter plastic ball has a smaller mass and simply bounces off the pins.

Archimedes

Archimedes (c.287–212 BC) was a Greek mathematician and inventor who studied forces and how they could be used by simple machines. He founded statics, discovered why objects float and sink, and worked out the principles behind levers and pulleys.

Newton's laws of motion

In 1687, English physicist Sir Isaac Newton devised three laws to summarize the principles of force and motion.

Force *Motion*

First law

An object continues in a state of rest or constant motion unless a force acts upon it. The inline skater in the picture will keep on rolling at the same speed until a force, such as friction, acts to stop him.

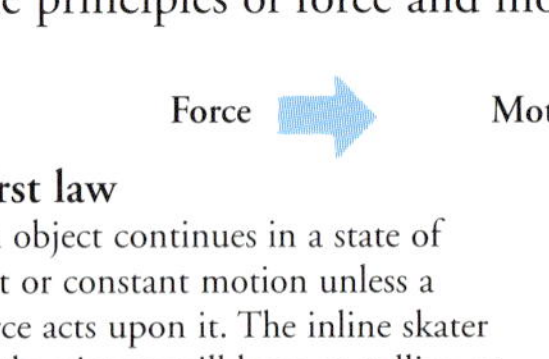

Second law

An object's acceleration is equal to the size of the force acting upon it divided by the object's mass. This inline skater's acceleration depends on how heavy he is and how hard he is pushed.

Third law

For every force there is an equal force acting in the opposite direction. Forces act in pairs, so when A pushes B, an equal and opposite force acts on A, making both inline skaters move apart.

Circular motion

A free-moving object will naturally move in a straight line. Centripetal force is needed for the object to move in a circle. This is a force that pulls an object towards the centre of a circle, constantly changing its direction and stopping it from moving off in a straight line. A motorcycle uses centripetal force to travel around a bend.

Friction between the tyres and the road provides centripetal force.

FIND OUT MORE FRICTION GRAVITY MACHINES, SIMPLE MAGNETISM PRESSURE

FORESTS

A THIRD OF THE WORLD'S land surface consists of forest – areas of land covered by dense tree cover. Each forest is an ecosystem – a group of animals and plants interacting with the physical environment and one another. More plants and animals live in forests than in any other environment. Forests differ according to the climate – boreal, temperate, or tropical. They help maintain the Earth's natural balance; trees absorb and release gases which regulate the climate.

Tropical forest
Temperate forest
Boreal coniferous forest

Tropical forest

Tropical forests, or rainforests, tend to thrive in warm and wet climates. The porous soil is generally rich in aluminium and iron. In one hectare there may be more than 200 species of trees, hundreds of birds, mammals, and reptiles, and thousands of insects.

Emergent trees rise up to 60 m (197 ft).

Canopy of trees 15 m (50 ft) above the ground

Plants twine around branches.

Understorey contains shrubs and young growth.

Tropical forest

Each forest has layers of vegetation. In a tropical forest emergent trees poke through the top. Below are the canopy, the understorey, and the forest floor.

Broad leaves of deciduous trees grow rapidly in summer, and are shed in winter.

Temperate forest

Down-angled branches allow the trees to shed the weight of the snow in cold climates without breaking them.

Forest floor is dark with little plant growth, but vegetation decay enriches the soil.

Temperate forest

These forests are found in mild or temperate climates, where winters are cool and summers are warm. The majority of trees are deciduous, such as oak and beech. Many temperate forests have been cleared for farmland because the soil beneath is very fertile.

Boreal coniferous forest

In cool, northern, or boreal regions, such as North Asia, there are vast areas of boreal forests, sometimes known as taiga. These dense forests contain hardy coniferous or evergreen trees, such as spruce, pine, fir, and larch trees.

Soil beneath these trees is acid and infertile.

Boreal coniferous forest

Afforestation

More people are becoming aware of the value of forests. In Southeast Asia, new forest land is created with tree-planting programmes. Some forests are now conservation areas.

Deforestation

Each year, forest land the size of Washington State, USA is destroyed. Trees are cut down for farmland or timber. Deforestation can cause huge environmental problems, disturbing the soil and forest life. Fewer trees to absorb carbon dioxide may also disrupt the climate.

Cattle ranching
Huge areas of rainforest in Brazil are cut down for cattle-ranching, which exhausts the soil within a few years.

Slash and burn
Nomadic farmers slash and burn forests for farmland. After a few years, they move on to allow the soil to regenerate.

Overgrazing
A shortage of land forces nomadic farmers to stay in one place. The land is over-grazed, and the soil dries up.

CLIMATE   ECOLOGY AND ECOSYSTEMS   PLANT USES   POLLUTION   RAINFOREST WILDLIFE   SOIL   TREES   WOODLAND WILDLIFE

FOSSILS

THE REMAINS AND TRACES of past life forms are called fossils. All living organisms are potential fossils, but only a few are preserved. The most common fossils are those of hard parts of animals and plants. Only rarely is soft tissue fossilized. Sometimes, trace fossils, such as footprints, are found. The study of fossils, called palaeontology, is crucial to our understanding of life.

Graptolite

Conodont

Fossil dating
Some fossils, such as graptolites and conodonts, evolved and became extinct over geologically short periods of time. This makes them useful for dating the rocks in which they are found.

How a fossil is formed

In order for something to fossilize, it must be buried quickly by sediment, such as sand or mud, before it decomposes. Fossils form in a variety of ways, depending on the environment in which the animal or plant lived, and the conditions after it was buried.

The skeleton may be broken up.

Water deposits sediment.

Erosion of the rock brings the fossils nearer the surface.

1 After death, the soft parts of a *Triceratops* decompose quickly, leaving just the hard skeleton and horns.

2 Through time, the bones are buried under thick layers of sediment and harden to form fossils.

3 The layers of sediment turn to rock. They may be pushed up or folded to form mountains.

4 Erosion exposes the bones. Palaeontologists can then collect and study the dinosaur remains.

Studying fossils

The study of the evolution of environments and natural communities is an important part of palaeontology. This limestone contains fossils of different animals, such as trilobites and corals. It shows a community that existed on the seafloor more than 400 million years ago.

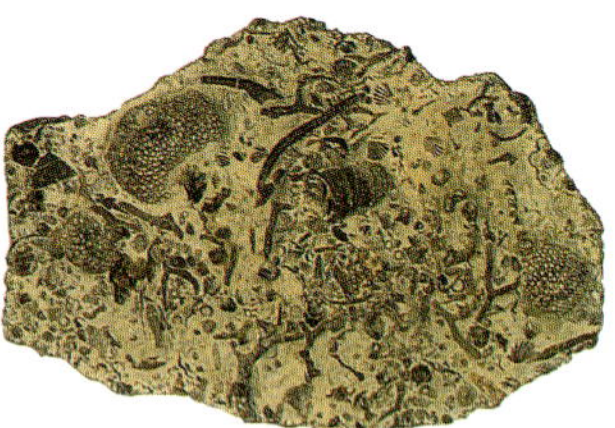

Limestone from Much Wenlock, England

Coral
Fossil corals are common because they have a hard skeleton. Soft-bodied animals, such as sea anemones and jellyfish, would have lived in the same community, but are unlikely to have fossilized.

Trilobite
Trilobites were arthropods that lived in the sea. They shed their shells regularly, as modern arthropods do, and these shells are often found as fossils. They are divided into three distinct parts, or lobes, hence the name "trilobite". A few fossils of soft parts have been found.

Types of fossil

Fossils range from microscopic plants and animals to the huge bones of dinosaurs. They can be almost unchanged from the original or replaced by minerals.

Amber
The fossilized resin of trees, called amber, often contains trapped insects and other small animals and plants. The trapped fossils are often preserved with much detail.

Volcanic ash
This child's body was buried by volcanic ash at Pompeii, Italy, in AD 79. Ash turns to rock quickly. A buried animal or plant may rot away to leave a hollow, which, if filled with plaster, forms a cast.

Trees
Fossilized trees, such as these *Lepidodendron* trunks and roots, can be preserved as internal moulds of the bark. The inside rots away and is replaced by sand.

Bones
Vertebrate fossils are made of many parts and are usually found as single pieces. If conditions are right, a skeleton can be preserved whole, as in this *Diplomystus*, an ancestor of the modern herring.

Females were larger than males.

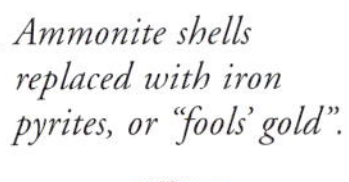

Ammonite shells replaced with iron pyrites, or "fools' gold".

Petrification
These monkey-puzzle cones have been turned to stone, or petrified. This happened when silica-rich waters crystallized within the cells of the cones.

Concretions
Hard lumps, or concretions, are often formed around fossils in sediments. This concretion reveals the fossil shell and mould of a clam.

Georges Cuvier

A French zoologist, Georges Cuvier (1769–1832) realized that the parts of the body were interrelated. For example, an animal that has hooves is a herbivore, and must have herbivore's teeth. He identified a fossil as a marsupial from a jaw.

Jurassic ammonite

Ammonites
These molluscs were abundant in the seas of the Mesozoic Era. Their shells were made of the mineral aragonite and were often replaced by other minerals during fossilization.

FIND OUT MORE   ARTHROPODS   DINOSAURS   EVOLUTION   GEOLOGY   PREHISTORIC LIFE

Fossils

Invertebrates

Raphidonema is a sponge from the warm waters of the Cretaceous Period.

Didymograptus are Ordovician graptolites. They floated in oceans.

Trachyphyllia is a Miocene solitary coral.

Lonsdaleia lived as a colony during the Carboniferous Period.

Lovenia is a heart urchin with a flattened shell.

Archaeogeryon is a deep-water Miocene mud crab.

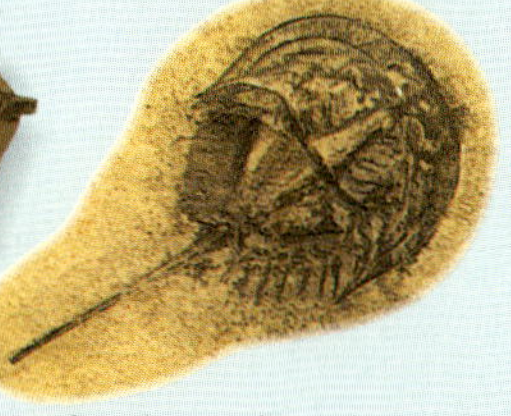

Mesolimulus is a horseshoe crab of the Jurassic and Cretaceous Periods. It has a horseshoe-shaped shell.

Viviparus is a freshwater snail.

A stalk attached the brachiopod to the sea floor.

Terebratula is a brachiopod, also known as a lamp shell.

Lingula is a brachiopod with a thin shell.

Stem made up of disc-like plates.

Dimerocrinites is a sea lily, or crinoid, from the Silurian and Devonian Periods.

Vertebrates

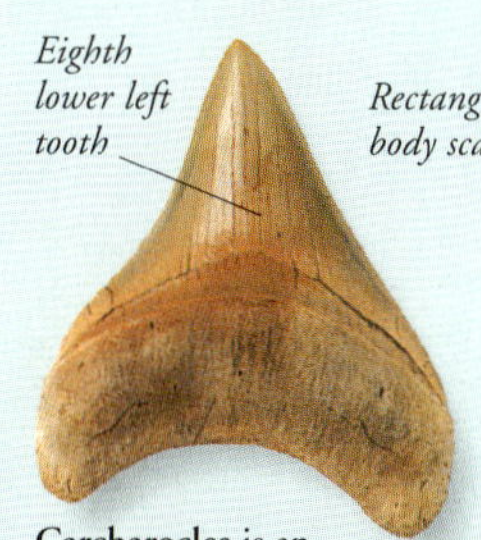

Eighth lower left tooth

Carcharocles is an extinct shark.

Rectangular body scales

Dapedium is a fish from the shallow seas of the late Triassic and Jurassic Periods.

Macrocranion from the Eocene Period resembles a living hedgehog without the spikes.

Pointed skull *Long hind leg*

Rana is a true frog that first appeared in the Eocene Period.

Raphus is a huge, extinct, flightless pigeon, commonly known as the dodo.

Nostril

Ichthyosaurus is a sea reptile of the Jurassic Period.

Ring of bones around the eye

Nostril

Dimetrodon is a mammal-like carnivorous reptile of the Permian Period.

Dagger-like teeth *Eye socket*

Plants

Collenia is an alga of the Precambrian and Cambrian Periods.

Stigmaria are the root-bearing branches of a Carboniferous club-moss.

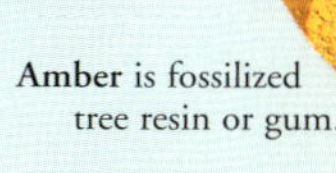

Amber is fossilized tree resin or gum.

Trapped spider

Ficus is a fig which first appeared in the Eocene Period.

Porana is a Miocene flower.

Populus is a poplar, almost identical to poplars today.

Growth rings

Quercus is oak. It first appeared in the Eocene Period.

Polished, petrified wood

Carved jet

Jet is a type of fossilized wood.

Ribbed seed

Trigonocarpus is the seed of a Carboniferous seed fern.

F

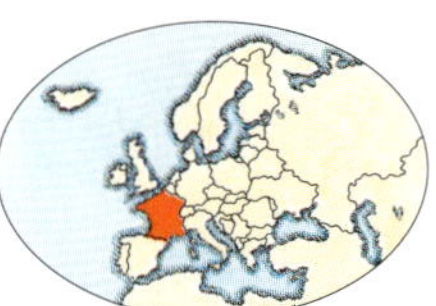

FRANCE

THE LARGEST COUNTRY in western Europe, France stretches from the Pyrenees in the south to the English Channel in the north. A founder member of the European Economic Community (now European Union), France plays a key role in world affairs. It is a leading industrial nation, although some five per cent of the population works in farming. The first of the modern republics, France includes Corsica, Guyana, and various islands in the Caribbean and Pacific Ocean.

River Seine

From its source in the east, the River Seine crosses Paris, before winding its way north to the Atlantic Ocean. France's river network, which also includes the Loire and the Rhône, is used for transport and for irrigating farmland.

The Seine in Normandy

Corsican *maquis*

Physical features

France's landscape varies from undulating fields in the north to sparse hills in the Massif Central, and mountains in the Alps and Pyrenees in the south.

Corsica

With an area of 8,630 sq km (3,350 sq miles), Corsica is the third largest Mediterranean island. Fragrant, thorny scrub called *maquis* covers the slopes of towering granite peaks, and rich fertile valleys are used to graze sheep and grow vines. The capital is Ajaccio.

Climate

Northwest France, particularly Brittany, is mild but damp. The east has hot summers and stormy winters. Summers in the south are dry and hot, and forest fires are common. In the Pyrenees and Alps, winter snowfalls are heavy, making these ideal areas for skiing.

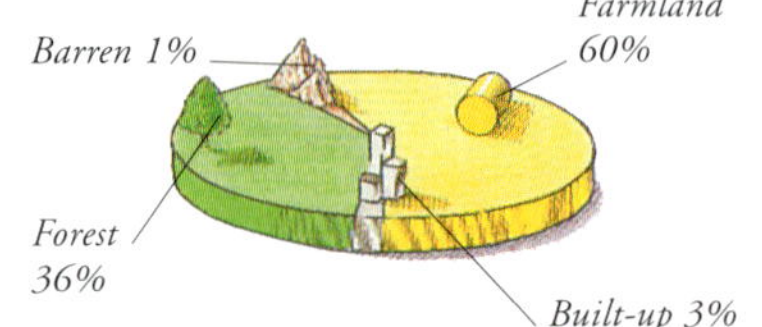

Land use

France's fertile farmland includes gently rolling pastures and fields of wheat and sugar beet in the north, and vineyards and lavender fields in the south. Much of the Massif Central is pasture land for grazing sheep.

Paris

The Louvre Museum lies on the fashionable Right Bank of the River Seine, which divides the city. The Left Bank is traditionally home to students, artists, and the famous Eiffel Tower. One of the world's most beautiful and most visited capitals, Paris is the cultural and political centre of France.

The Louvre Museum

People

People of French descent make up about 94 per cent of the population. Among these are several groups who speak their own languages and have strong independence movements. These include the Bretons of Brittany in the north, about 500,000 Basques in the Pyrenees, and the Corsicans.

107 per sq km
(278 per sq mile)

75%
Urban

25%
Rural

Ethnic groups
France's five million immigrants include mainly North African Muslims and economic migrants from South and Central Europe. Most live and work in the cities.

Leisure

Football, rugby, cycling, and tennis are all popular sports in France, as are horseracing and Formula 1. The French Open is a major international tennis championship.

Tour de France
Each year, more than a hundred of the world's leading professional cyclists compete in this famous cycle race over a 3,400-km (2,113-mile) route in 24 one-day stages.

Boules
Throughout France, groups of people playing *boules* are a common sight in the town or village square. *Boules* is France's national game and involves rolling heavy balls at a smaller target ball.

Farming

The French grow a variety of crops, such as wheat, barley, sugar beet, and grapes for making wine. About a third of all the farmland is pasture for grazing cows and sheep, which are reared for milk to make dairy products, and for meat.

Cantal

Livarot

St.-Nectaire

Cheese
France produces more than 365 kinds of cheese, from cow, sheep, and goats' milk. These include St.-Nectaire, Cantal, and Livarot, and the famous Brie, Camembert, and Roquefort. Milk and butter are also important exports.

Cereals
France's main cereal crop is wheat, which grows on large farms in the north of France where the soil is good.

Wine
The wines of Bordeaux, Burgundy, Champagne, and the Rhône valley are sold worldwide. France is the leading producer and controls quality strictly.

Food

French cuisine is world famous, and words such as café, restaurant, paté, and quiche are common in many languages. Special French dishes include *bouillabaisse* (fish soup), *escargots* (snails), and *grenouilles* (frogs' legs).

Industry

France has strong chemical, steel, electronics, and manufacturing industries, and an active aerospace programme. Nuclear power provides three-quarters of the country's electricity. Perfume and fashion are also a major source of income.

Car production
Most French drivers buy French cars, such as this Renault Espace. Other makes include Peugeot and Citroën. The French car industry ranks fourth in the world.

Transport

France boasts the world's fastest train, the TGV, which can travel at speeds of up to 300 kmh (186 mph). A direct service now runs to England via the Channel Tunnel.

Perfume
French perfumes, such as Chanel, are world famous. Many are made from the fragrant oils extracted from roses, jasmine, and lavender that grow in the southeast of the country.

Tourism
The fashionable resorts of the Côte d'Azur in southeast France attract thousands of tourists every summer. France is now the world's leading tourist destination, attracting 75 million visitors each year.

Monaco

This tiny independent principality on the Côte d'Azur derives its income from tourism, banking, sales tax, and gambling. It has close ties with France.

Grand Casino
The people of Monaco pay very little tax and earn more per head than any other country in the world. The gaming rooms and roulette wheels of the Grand Casino in Monte Carlo are open to anyone with money to spend.

MONACO FACTS

CAPITAL CITY Monaco

AREA 1.95 sq km (0.75 sq miles)

POPULATION 31,700

MAIN LANGUAGE French

MAJOR RELIGION Christian

CURRENCY Euro

FIND OUT MORE — CARS AND TRUCKS · CLOTHES AND FASHION · CYCLING · EMPIRES · EUROPE, HISTORY OF · EUROPEAN UNION · FARMING · FRANCE, HISTORY OF · TRADE AND INDUSTRY · TRAINS AND RAILWAYS

FRANCE, HISTORY OF

THE LARGEST COUNTRY in western Europe, France has dominated European history ever since the Franks conquered the country in the 5th century. Its vast natural wealth and large population have enabled a succession of rulers, such as Charlemagne in the 9th century, Louis XIV in the 17th, and Napoleon in the 19th, to create powerful empires that spanned Europe. Despite three bitter wars with Germany between 1870 and 1945, France emerged as one of the world's superpowers. Today, France is a leading member of the European Union, and one of the wealthiest countries in the world.

Horses heads, carved c.10,000 BC

Prehistoric France

The first inhabitants of France were prolific artists. More than 20,000 years ago, they adorned caves at Lascaux and elsewhere with lifelike pictures of animals. They also carved likenesses of animal heads from bone, antler, and rock.

Samian ware bowl

French potters made this type of ware in the Roman period.

Roman France

Between 58 and 51 BC, a Roman army led by Julius Caesar conquered France. The new province of Gaul was one of the richest in the empire. Trade flourished, and the Romans built many roads and bridges. They also introduced growing grapes for wine.

Franks

In 486, the Franks from Germany routed the last Roman governor of Gaul and took control, giving France its name. At first the Franks continued with Roman customs, but their empire broke up in civil wars. The 8th-century kings Charles Martel, Pepin the Short, and Charlemagne restored order.

Charlemagne

Medieval France

In common with other European rulers, the power of the French kings was always limited by the strength of local nobles. Despite this weakness, France became one of the richest countries in Europe during the 11th century. Major trade fairs in the Champagne region attracted merchants from all over Europe, and trade and commerce flourished.

Angevin Empire

As a result of marriage and war, Henry II of England (r.1154–89) ruled much of western and northern France. His vast realm was called the Angevin Empire, after the county of Anjou. For years it was a threat to French unification.

Château Gaillard, an Angevin castle

Religious wars

The Reformation split France, with many Catholics becoming Huguenots (Protestants). In 1562, civil war broke out between the two sides; religious toleration was agreed by the Edict of Nantes in 1598, but tension remained high. In 1685, Louis XIV revoked the Edict, and many Huguenots fled to England and Holland.

Renaissance France

Joan of Arc, who fought the English for independence, was burnt at the stake in 1431. During the 15th century, the French kings drove out the English, and united their country. They also crushed the power of the nobles. During the next century, the ideas of the Italian Renaissance entered France. New châteaux were built, and the arts flourished.

Golden age

The 17th and 18th centuries were a golden age of the arts. Royal support led to the founding of the Gobelins tapestry works in 1602 and the royal pottery at Sèvres in 1756. The nobility supported artists such as Watteau and Fragonard, dramatists such as Racine, Molière and Corneille, the writer Montaigne, creator of the essay, and the fable-writer La Fontaine.

Bourbons

Under the Bourbon kings, France emerged as the major power in Europe during the 17th century. Habsburg-ruled Spain and Austria – enemies of France – were defeated, and all power was centralized under the king. Industry and commerce were supported, and France established colonies in North America and India.

Palace of Versailles

In order to increase his own power, and reduce that of the nobility, Louis XIV built this vast new palace outside Paris. Some 36,000 people worked on the building, decorating it with the best examples of French art and design. At the centre was the king's bed chamber, where Louis received guests.

Hand-painted figures

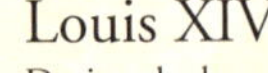

Gilded decoration

Sèvres porcelain vase

Louis XIV

During the long reign of Louis XIV (r.1643–1715), the power of the French kings reached its height. Louis believed in the divine right of kings to rule, and governed without parliament. He reorganized the army and expanded French territory. But his lavish lifestyle left France almost bankrupt.

F

French Revolution

Revolution broke out in 1789, sweeping away the king and nobility. A new National Assembly was set up, and swore the famous tennis court oath, that they would not disband until France had a proper constitution. Napoleon Bonaparte became Emperor in 1804, marking the end of the revolutionary period.

Monarchy and empire

After the defeat of Napoleon in 1815, France had a series of short-lived, weak governments. The restored Bourbon monarchy was overthrown in 1830 and King Louis Philippe lost his throne in 1848. The resulting Second Republic collapsed when its president, Louis-Napoleon (r.1852–70), became emperor. In spite of these problems, France grew prosperous.

Revolution of 1848

In February 1848, Parisians rose up against their ineffectual king, Louis Philippe. A republic was set up, with Louis-Napoleon, a nephew of Bonaparte, as president. Radical reforms were promised, but in 1852 Napoleon became emperor.

Revolutionaries in Paris, 1848

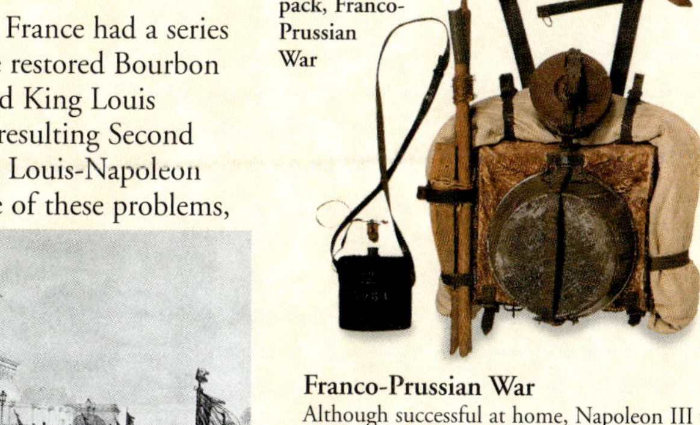

Infantryman's pack, Franco-Prussian War

Franco-Prussian War

Although successful at home, Napoleon III was no match for Bismarck, chancellor of Prussia. In 1870, rivalry between France and Prussia led to war, but the French armies were unprepared and were soon defeated. France lost the provinces of Alsace and Lorraine to Germany.

Third Republic

The Third Republic (1870–1940) was riven with internal disputes and conflicts between moderates, radicals, socialists, and royalists. Between 1918 and its collapse in 1940, there were 44 governments and 20 different prime ministers. Yet France stayed one of the leading states in Europe, with a worldwide empire and a strong economy.

J'Accuse, writer Emile Zola's pamphlet supporting Dreyfus

Dreyfus case

In October 1894, French army captain Alfred Dreyfus was court-martialled for treason, for passing military secrets to Germany. But a mistake had been made, and a campaign to free Dreyfus began. He was cleared in 1906, but the case split the nation between his supporters and those who refused to change the verdict.

Vichy France

In 1940, German forces invaded France. French general and right-wing politician Marshal Pétain set up a government in Vichy, central France. This government collaborated with the occupying forces; opposition was led from London by Charles de Gaulle, leader of the Free French. Vichy France was occupied by the Germans in 1942.

Modern France

After the liberation of France from German occupation in 1944, a Fourth Republic was set up to govern the country. Like its predecessor, it was weak and was brought down by the unrest caused by the Algerian war in 1958. Charles de Gaulle then set up the Fifth Republic, aiming to restore French prestige and prosperity.

May 1968

In May 1968, students demanding more money for education demonstrated against high defence spending. Riots broke out in Paris and elsewhere, with fighting between police and students. A general strike ensued, and de Gaulle's government was weakened.

After the riots, Paris, May 1968

Charles de Gaulle

Charles de Gaulle (1890–1970) trained as a soldier, rising to command an armoured division. On the fall of France in 1940, he fled to Britain and called on French people to resist German occupation. As leader of the Free French, he did much to boost French morale during the war. In 1958 he became president, leading his country until he resigned in 1969.

Algerian war

In 1954, Algeria, one of several African countries colonized by France, demanded that it be granted its independence. This led to conflict with the many European settlers in the country. The French army supported the settlers in their wish to remain French and waged a vicious war against the Algerian rebels. Algeria finally won its independence in 1962.

Cross of Lorraine | Flag of the Free French

Timeline

58–51 BC Gaul (present-day France) becomes part of the Roman Empire.

AD 486 The Franks take control of the country.

1337–1453 France and Britain fight the Hundred Years' War.

Encyclopedie, 1751

1589 Henry IV becomes first Bourbon king.

1643–1715 France reaches height of its power under Louis XIV.

1789 Revolution breaks out in Paris.

1848 After a revolution, the short-lived Second Republic is established.

1870–71 Third Republic set up.

1870s Impressionist movement founded by Claude Monet and other French painters.

Claude Monet, *Waterlilies*

1914–18 France fights Germany in World War I.

1946 Fourth Republic established after World War II.

1958 De Gaulle takes power and introduces Fifth Republic.

1950s–90s France is a leading member of European Union,

FIND OUT MORE   EUROPE, HISTORY OF   FRENCH REVOLUTION   GERMANY, HISTORY OF   MEDIEVAL EUROPE   NAPOLEON BONAPARTE   NAPOLEONIC WARS   ROMAN EMPIRE   WORLD WAR I   WORLD WAR II

FRANKLIN, BENJAMIN

INVENTOR, PRINTER, PUBLISHER, writer, scientist, politician, diplomat, and an author of both the US Declaration of Independence and the US Constitution – there was nothing Benjamin Franklin did not turn his hand to.

He was born into a poor family, but had a fertile mind very receptive to new ideas. He invented items such as the lightning conductor and bifocal lenses, but he is most respected for his contribution to the founding of the USA. He is sometimes known as the "wisest American."

Early life

Benjamin Franklin was born in 1706 in the American port of Boston. He was the son of a candle and soap maker, and left school at age 10 to help in his father's business. Later he worked for his half brother James, printer and publisher of a newspaper to which Benjamin contributed. After disagreements with James, he left Boston in 1723 to work as a printer in Philadelphia.

Printer

Franklin prospered as a printer. As publisher of the popular *Poor Richard's Almanac* between 1732–57, he introduced numerous common-sense sayings that have since become part of the American language. He also set up an academy that later became the University of Pennsylvania.

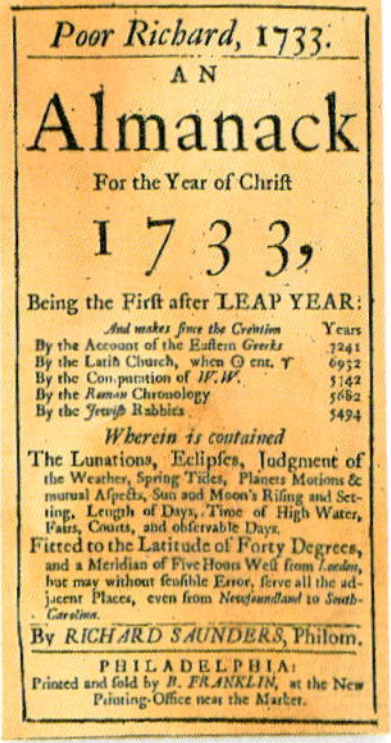

Bend caused by lightning.

Scientist

In 1748, Franklin handed over his printing business to his foreman so that he could devote his life to science. He researched the nature of electricity, and this work led to his invention of the lightning rod, that protects tall buildings from lightning. He also worked out a theory of heat absorption and tracked the paths of storms across the sky.

Lightning

In 1752, Franklin flew a kite in a thunderstorm to prove that lightning is electrical. Electricity from the thunderclouds flowed down the string to a metal key tied on it near the ground. Sparks flew from the key, showing the presence of the electrical charge in the sky.

Franklin experimenting with a kite and lightning

Inventor

Franklin was a tireless inventor, using his scientific knowledge to devise a number of inventions that were designed to make human life safer and more comfortable. These ranged from bifocal eyeglasses – combining two lenses of different strengths in one frame to correct both close and distant vision – to a musical glass "armonica." Among his useful inventions were the lightning rod and an energy-saving stove still made today.

The armonica was played by rubbing the fingers gently on the edges of the glasses.

Stove

Among Franklin's many inventions was a practical stove that made use of the heat that would otherwise have escaped up the chimney. Stoves like this were installed in many American houses.

Armonica

In the early 1760s, Franklin built a musical instrument made up of a series of glass bowls, graduated in size and fitted one inside another. By rotating a spindle the edges of the bowls passed through a trough of water. Contact with the musician's fingertips produced a penetrating sound. Composers such as Mozart and Beethoven wrote music for this strange device.

Statesman

During the American Revolution, Franklin was a member of the committee that wrote the Declaration of Independence, which he signed in 1776. Later that year, he sailed to France to win diplomatic recognition for the new nation. When the war ended, he was one of the main US negotiators in the peace talks.

Franklin (left) talks to the French king and queen (seated, right) and members of their court.

Constitution

In 1787, Franklin helped to write the new American constitution. Although his proposal for a single-chamber congress was rejected, he negotiated a compromise between the different authors that resulted in the constitution that survives today.

BENJAMIN FRANKLIN

1706	Born in Boston, MA.
1723	Begins work as a printer.
1732–57	Publishes *Poor Richard's Almanac*.
1752	Conducts famous experiment with lightning.
1776	Helps to draft Declaration of Independence.
1781	Chosen as one of the US negotiators with Britain.
1787	Member of group that draws up US constitution.
1790	Dies in Philadelphia.

FIND OUT MORE   AMERICAN REVOLUTION   ELECTRICITY   EYES AND VISION   GOVERNMENTS AND POLITICS   INVENTIONS   MUSICAL INSTRUMENTS   UNITED STATES, HISTORY OF

FRENCH REVOLUTION

IN 1789, REVOLUTION BROKE OUT in France when people rose up against poverty and injustice. The French Revolution swept away the power of the monarchy and ended the traditional social order. When the revolution began, poverty was widespread, the king was unpopular, and people resented the clergy and nobility. Following the formation of the National Assembly, France was declared a republic, the king was executed, and, for a while, terror reigned. In 1799, Napoleon came to power, and the revolution ended.

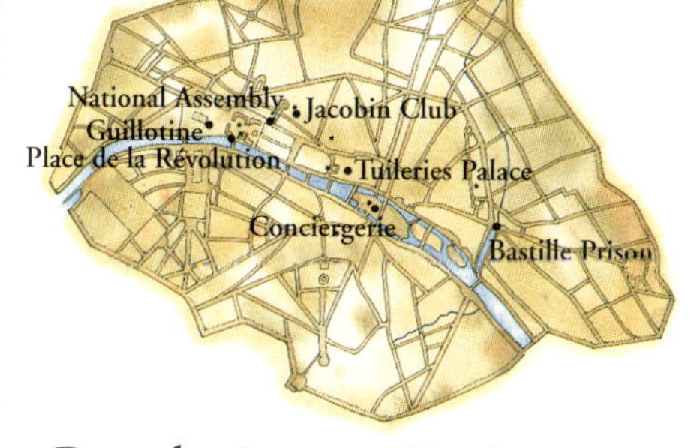

Revolutionary Paris

The key events of the revolution occurred on the streets of Paris. Various political groups sprang up, such as the Jacobin Club, which relied on the Parisian *sans culottes* for support.

National Assembly

In 1788, France ran out of money, and King Louis XVI called the Estates General, representing clergy, nobility, and middle classes. The Third Estate formed a National Assembly, seized lands, and drew up a new constitution.

Rights of Man

The National Assembly issued the *Declaration of the Rights of Man and the Citizen*, stating that "Men are born and remain equal". Women's rights were not included, but the ideals of "liberty, equality, and fraternity" inspired everyone.

Storming of the Bastille

In 1789, angry demonstrators seized the Bastille, a prison that had been a symbol of oppression for many years. This act sparked a wave of rebellion. Outside Paris, peasants attacked the country houses of the nobility they hated.

Reign of Terror

By 1792, the revolution was under threat. There were food shortages, royalist uprisings in the countryside, and a threat by Prussia to invade and restore the monarchy. Extremists, known as Jacobins, grew in power, declaring a republic and executing the king in 1793. They set up the Committee of Public Safety, and a reign of terror began. Anyone suspected of being an enemy of the revolution was arrested and guillotined. Thousands died. By 1794, the leaders of the Committee were themselves executed, and the terror was over.

Revolutionaries

The revolutionaries were men and women from all social classes: lawyers, peasants, workers. Street revolutionaries were known as *sans culottes* (without breeches) because they wore striped trousers. Two rival revolutionary groups emerged: the Girondins and the more radical Jacobins.

Guillotine

Named after a French doctor, the guillotine consisted of a wooden frame, with a sharp blade mounted on it, which sliced off the victims' heads. This killing machine was quicker than previous methods of execution, and was, therefore, thought to be more humane.

Sharpened blade fell on victims' necks.

Robespierre

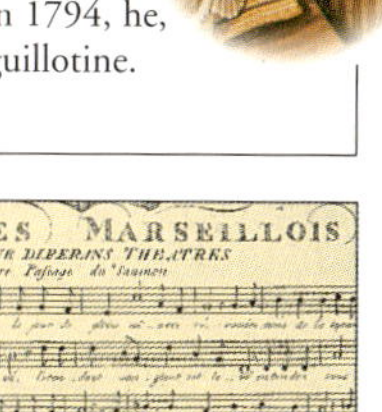

A lawyer by profession, Maximilien Robespierre (1758–94) was one of the leaders of the revolution. He headed the Jacobin Club, and, by 1793, was leader of the Committee of Public Safety that conducted the Reign of Terror. In 1794, he, too, went to the guillotine.

Marseillaise

From 1792, revolution spread outside French borders. A soldier composed the *Marseillaise* as a revolutionary marching song. It is now France's national anthem.

The bonnet rouge, or red bonnet, symbolized freedom. It looked like the cap worn by freed Roman slaves.

Coarse working blouse

White was the colour of the royal family.

Red and blue were the colours of Paris.

Striped trousers

Strong leather shoes

Timeline

1788 France bankrupt. Louis XVI summons Estates General.

May 1789 Third Estate forms National Assembly.

Louis XVI

14 July, 1789 Paris mob storms the Bastille; French Revolution begins.

27 August, 1789 National Assembly issues *Rights of Man.*

October 1789 Women march to Versailles from Paris to demand bread.

1791 The French revolution inspires a slave rebellion in Haiti.

1792 National Assembly abolishes monarchy. France becomes a republic and goes to war with Austria and Prussia.

1793 Louis XVI executed. Counter-revolution breaks out. Revolutionary war spreads across Europe.

1793–4 Reign of Terror.

1795 The Directory, a more moderate board of governors, is formed and takes power.

1799 Napoleon overthrows Directory and takes power.

1798–99 Revolution inspires uprisings in Ireland.

FIND OUT MORE — AMERICAN REVOLUTION · EUROPE, HISTORY OF · FRANCE, HISTORY OF · GOVERNMENTS AND POLITICS · NAPOLEONIC WARS

FREUD, SIGMUND

ONE HUNDRED YEARS AGO, people viewed the workings of the human mind as a great mystery. Sigmund Freud helped to make sense of that mystery. Because of his innovative ideas, he is often known as the father of psychiatry. Freud was an Austrian doctor who worked in Vienna almost all his life. He researched the meaning of dreams, how the unconscious mind works, and how events in our past influence the actions we take. In developing the science of psychoanalysis, he provided insights that have affected every aspect of modern life.

Early life

Freud was born into a Jewish family in 1856 in Freiburg (Pribor), in what is now the Czech Republic. In 1859 his family moved to Vienna. Freud was a brilliant student, coming top of his class in school for six years. In 1873 he began to study medicine at Vienna, and in 1881 he qualified as a doctor.

Freud's couch

Psychoanalysis

In 1886, Freud began to specialise in neuroses, or nervous diseases. To find out what was causing his patients' illnesses, he used first hypnotism and then free association – instructing his patients to say whatever came into their head in the belief that they would reveal the cause of their illness. Freud published his ideas in 1895 in *Studies on Hysteria*, the first-ever account of psychoanalysis – the interpretation and treatment of mental disorders.

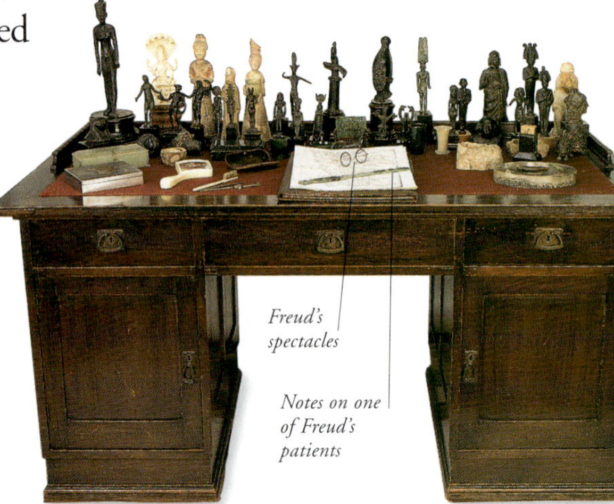

Freud's spectacles

Notes on one of Freud's patients

Analyst's couch

Much of Freud's work consisted of listening to his patients as they talked about themselves. The patient lay on a couch in Freud's study, and Freud sat at his desk, surrounded by his collection of ancient Egyptian statues, listening and taking notes. This technique, devised by Freud, is still used widely today. Many of Freud's books are made up largely of case studies – reports of the psychoanalytic sessions and the conclusions Freud drew from them.

The Psychopathology of Everyday Life (1904)

Chair is made in the shape of a person.

Freud's chair

The Interpretation of Dreams (1900)

Interpretation of dreams

Freud believed that beneath our conscious mind is a submerged unconscious that governs much of our behaviour. Dreams are the way in which the unconscious comes to the surface. He published this theory in *The Interpretation of Dreams* in 1900.

Freudian slips

In his book *The Psychopathology of Everyday Life* (1904), Freud explained how slips of the tongue can reveal hidden, unconscious wishes. Freud made many connections between what we say and do and what we actually mean.

International Psychoanalytical Association

Early in his career, Freud attracted intense hostility to his work, but gradually his ideas were accepted. In 1902, he established a psychoanalytical society in Vienna, and in 1910 he set up the International Psychoanalytical Association (IPA) to promote his ideas. Regular IPA meetings and discussions helped Freud confirm his theories about the mind and spread them to a wider audience.

Carl Gustav Jung

The Swiss psychiatrist CG Jung (1875–1961) and Freud lectured together in the USA in 1909. Jung was the first president of the IPA, but resigned in 1914 because he disagreed with Freud about the origins of neurosis. He later created his own school of thought about the mind's workings.

Later life

In the 1920s, Freud developed a new theory that the mind is made up of three parts – the id, which contains impulses, the ego, which represents reasoning, and the superego, the self-critical area. He was developing this theory when he left Austria in 1938 because it was occupied by Nazi Germany.

Anna Freud

In 1938, Freud moved to London, where he died in exile the following year. His work was carried on by his youngest daughter, Anna (1895–1982). A qualified teacher, she specialized in child psychiatry. She founded and directed a world-famous clinic for child therapy in London and wrote several books.

FIND OUT MORE

BRAIN AND NERVOUS SYSTEM · GERMANY, HISTORY OF · HOSPITALS · MEDICINE · MEDICINE, HISTORY OF

FRICTION

DRAGGING A HEAVY OBJECT across the floor is difficult because of friction, a force that opposes motion. Friction occurs between any two surfaces that are in contact, because even seemingly smooth surfaces have microscopic ridges and troughs that make them grip one another. Friction is greater between rough surfaces than smooth ones. Static friction stops surfaces at rest from moving. Dynamic friction slows down surfaces in motion.

Static friction

Friction acts between these two masses and the wooden slope. Static friction on the stationary block is great enough to prevent it from moving. The moving block has overcome static friction, but it then produces dynamic friction, which limits its speed.

Gravity makes the mass on the smooth surface overcome static friction and slide down the slope.

Smooth surface

Rough surface

The rougher surface increases the force of static friction and prevents the mass from sliding.

Using friction

Friction can be useful. Without friction, no one would be able to walk or run. Friction helps people's shoes grip the ground and stops their feet from sliding out from under them. In the same way, friction enables a vehicle's tyres to grip the road. Most brakes use friction to slow a vehicle down. Friction between surfaces always produces heat, and sometimes electricity.

The pattern on the soles of these shoes is designed to create friction to give maximum grip.

Balloon charged by friction

Disc brakes

When the rider of this motorcycle applies the brakes, a pad presses against the metal disc fixed to the wheel. The rubbing action of the pad against the moving disc produces friction and slows the wheel enough to stop the motorcycle.

Brake pad unit

Disc

The brakes glow as the racing car slows down.

Friction and electricity

Rubbing two objects together can produce a charge of static electricity. Friction between a T-shirt and a balloon will dislodge negatively charged electrons from the atoms of the shirt. The electrons transfer to atoms in the balloon and give it a negative charge, while the shirt becomes positively charged. Opposite charges attract, so the negatively charged balloon clings to the positively charged shirt.

Friction and heat

In cold weather people often rub their hands together to warm them. Friction between two surfaces always produces heat. When a racing car brakes at high speed, the brakes glow red as the energy of the car's movement is changed into heat.

Reducing friction

If two moving machine parts rub together, friction will eventually damage them. Friction in machines generates heat and wastes a great deal of energy. Most methods of reducing friction involve keeping the surfaces apart in some way.

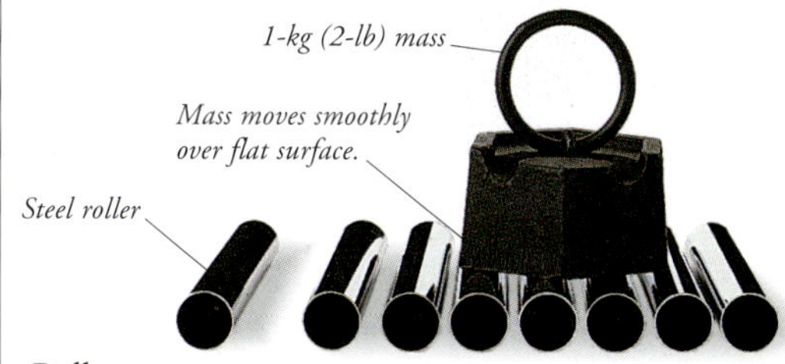

1-kg (2-lb) mass

Mass moves smoothly over flat surface.

Steel roller

Rollers

The rollers under this 1-kg (2-lb) mass allow it to move smoothly over a flat surface. The mass and the surface are not in contact, so there is no friction between them. If the mass is pushed or pulled, the rollers will roll instead of dragging over the surface.

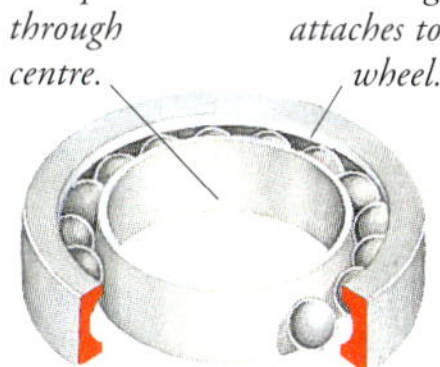

Axle passes through centre.

Outer ring attaches to wheel.

Ball bearing

A ball bearing is a device used to reduce friction between a wheel and its axle. As the wheel turns, the steel balls in the bearing roll around and prevent the wheel and axle from rubbing together.

Lubrication

Using a fluid such as oil to make machine parts move more smoothly and reduce wear is called lubrication. The oil coats the surfaces of the moving parts, preventing them from rubbing together.

Air resistance

Dynamic friction between the air and a moving object is called air resistance. Streamlining gives an object a smooth shape so that air flows more easily around it. Here, smoke trails blown over a streamlined car show how the air moves over its surface.

Hovercraft

A hovercraft overcomes the problem of friction by using high-pressure air as a lubricant. Fans pump air from the atmosphere into a flexible skirt around the craft's hull. This powerful downward jet of air allows the craft to hover over the water, reducing friction with the water's surface to a minimum. Large propellers on top of the craft move it quickly across the water.

Christopher Cockerell

In 1953, English engineer Christopher Cockerell (1910–99) began working on ways to reduce the friction between a ship's hull and the water. His solution was to lift the vessel above the water on a cushion of compressed air. In 1959, after making successful models, he produced the world's first practical hovercraft, called the SR-N1.

FROGS AND TOADS

THE CROAKING SOUNDS of frogs and toads are often heard in spring as they try to attract a mate. Frogs and toads are amphibians – cold-blooded animals that live both on land and in water. In Europe, they are easy to distinguish – frogs have slimy skins and live mainly in the water; toads have dry, warty skins and live mainly on land. In the tropics, they are more diverse and harder to tell apart. There are more than 2,600 species of frog and toad, living in most parts of the world where there is fresh water. Their habitats range from lakes and marshes, to rainforests, mountains, and deserts.

Features of frogs and toads

Frogs and toads have porous skin – water and air can pass through it – enabling them to breathe through their skin as well as their lungs. Most have sharp teeth, and can see and hear well. They have four legs, varying in length between species. Frogs range in size from a few centimetres long to the West African Goliath frog, which is 40 cm (16 in) in length. Some unusual species are the hairy frog – the male grows hair in the breeding season – and the Borneo flying frog that glides between trees.

Feeding

Most tadpoles are herbivorous, while adult frogs and toads are insectivorous or carnivorous. Prey includes insects, worms, spiders, fish, other frogs, or small reptiles, depending on species. Most species catch insects with their long sticky tongues. Larger frogs and toads rely on ambush. Giant horned toads and bullfrogs have powerful jaws and wide mouths and can even eat mice.

Sticky tongue is used to catch the worm.

Green toad

Warty skin

Short legs for hopping

Feet push off from the ground.

Hind legs in full stretch

Frog in a streamlined position in mid-flight

Eyes closed for protection

Webbed feet

Frogs swim by pulling their hind legs towards their bodies, then kicking them backwards, so pushing themselves forwards through the water.

Leaping and swimming

Long-legged frogs, such as this Northern leopard frog, can jump more than 30 times their own length in a single leap. When swimming, its long webbed toes help propel it through the water. Short-legged frogs walk, crawl, or do short hops. Some species, such as spade-foot frogs, have feet that can burrow into loose earth. Toads usually have short legs and can only hop weakly or walk. Some species, such as the natterjack toad, can run.

Back legs are long and very powerful.

Front legs are held back.

Northern leopard frog

Frogs use their front legs like brakes when they enter the water.

Reproduction

Most frogs and toads mate in water. The male fertilizes the eggs externally as the female lays them; a few species fertilize eggs internally. Some bear live young; others form "mating-balls" of a female and several males. The eggs develop into tadpoles that live in water and breathe through gills. The tadpoles change into air-breathing adults with lungs.

The dark dots develop into tadpoles.

The eggs stick together.

Tadpole uses its tail to swim.

Tiny buds from which front legs will grow.

Back legs

Tail eventually disappears.

Life-cycle of a common frog

1 Eggs stick together to form frogspawn. Each egg contains a dark centre that will become a tadpole. Many eggs are infertile and die, or are attacked by fungus or predators.

2 The newly hatched tadpole lives in the water and breathes through external gills. Most species at this stage are herbivorous and feed on plants.

3 By 6–9 weeks, the tadpole has grown considerably in size. The hind legs have developed. The tadpole now prepares to metamorphose, or change, into a froglet.

4 At 12 weeks, the tail has almost receded. The tadpole has become a froglet. It is now ready to leave the water to begin its adult life – partly on land.

Croaking

Frogs and toads croak to attract mates. Normally, it is the males that croak, using inflatable vocal sacs in the throat. Each species has its own distinctive croak so that the calls of the male only attract females of the same species. This avoids mating between different species in regions where there are many similar frogs and toads.

Painted reed frog

Vocal sac

Defence

Some frogs have poisonous skin that they advertise with bright colours. Others such as tree frogs may secrete bad-tasting sticky substances. Many toads, including cane toads, have poison-secreting glands. Large species, such as horned toads, give painful bites.

Poison dart frog

This South American frog is the most poisonous frog in the world. Its bright skin warns predators that it is poisonous to eat.

Skin is highly toxic.

Golden poison dart frog

Red belly

Fire-bellied toad

Fire-bellied toads in Europe have drab backs but bright red bellies. If threatened, the toad exposes its belly. This flash of colour frightens away predators.

Tree frogs

Tree frogs move with ease within trees. They have sticky discs on their toes and an opposing thumb enabling them to grip most objects, even smooth surfaces. Flying frogs are tree frogs with very large webbed feet that enable them to glide downwards from branch to branch.

Sticky pads on their toes enable them to grip branches.

Red-eyed tree frog

NORTHERN LEOPARD FROG

SCIENTIFIC NAME *Rana pipiens*

ORDER Anura

FAMILY Ranidae

DISTRIBUTION Northern and western USA and Canada, as far south as New Mexico

HABITAT Found in most habitats, even those far from water, which explains its other name of "meadow frog"

DIET Insects

SIZE Length 9–11 cm (3.5–4.5 in)

LIFESPAN Up to 6 years (in captivity)

FIND OUT MORE · AMPHIBIANS · CONSERVATION · EGGS · LAKE AND RIVER WILDLIFE · MARSH AND SWAMP WILDLIFE · POISONOUS ANIMALS · RAINFOREST WILDLIFE · URBAN WILDLIFE · WOODLAND WILDLIFE

Frogs

Asian painted frogs are burrowers that emerge onto the surface at night and inflate themselves if touched.

Foam-nesting frogs lay eggs in self-made foam in trees above water, into which the tadpoles drop.

Tomato frogs from Madagascar live on land, but breed in slow-moving or stagnant water.

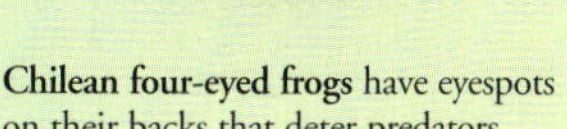

Chilean four-eyed frogs have eyespots on their backs that deter predators.

Malayan flying frogs cannot fly, but glide downwards.

Yellow and black poison dart frogs live in cracks in riverside rocks.

Paradoxical frogs develop from tadpoles twice their length and shrink as they "grow".

Green and black poison dart frogs have toxic skin.

Golden mantellas are poisonous frogs from Madagascar. They feed on small invertebrates.

African bullfrogs are large, carnivorous frogs that feed on other frogs, reptiles, and even mice and rats.

Common frogs are becoming rarer, partly due to the loss of wetland areas.

White's tree frogs are large Australian frogs.

Toads

Asian tree toads have flat digital discs, enabling them to climb riverside trees.

Natterjack toads, also called running toads, are the rarest toads in Britain.

Male midwife toads carry their eggs on their backs until they hatch into the water.

Asian horned toads resemble dried leaves, to escape discovery on the forest floor.

African clawed toads are totally aquatic.

Ornate horned toads from Argentina are large, aggressive toads with huge appetites.

Cane toads were introduced to Australia to control sugar cane pests, but have become pests themselves.

Mexican burrowing toads live in dry areas, rarely emerging onto the surface.

FRUITS AND SEEDS

CHERRIES, TOMATOES, and pea pods are all fruits. A fruit is the part of a plant that contains and protects the seeds. A fruit forms after a flower has been pollinated. First the petals wither and fall, then the part of the flower called the ovary swells. This becomes the fruit, containing one or several seeds, which are the plant's way of reproducing itself. Inside the fruit, the seeds are supplied with nutrients through tiny stalks connecting them to the fruit wall. As the seeds grow, the fruit ripens. Some fruits are sweet and juicy and may be edible; others are inedible, or even poisonous.

Parts of a fruit

In some fruits, the fruit wall, or pericarp, has three distinct layers – an outer epicarp, a middle mesocarp, and a hard, inner endocarp. These layers are easy to see in fleshy fruits, such as plums, but in other fruits the layers are not so clear. The fleshy part of an apple, for example, is actually formed from the receptacle – the swollen tip of the flower stem.

Remains of stamen

Pedicel (flower stalk)

Seed or pip (surrounded by endocarp)

Raspberries are made of clusters of drupelets.

Mesocarp

Epicarp (skin)

Receptacle

Drupelet

Raspberry

Cross-section of a raspberry

How a fruit develops

Once a flower has been pollinated and fertilization has taken place, its ovary becomes known as a fruit. This fruit and the tiny seeds within begin to develop and grow. Graduall y the fruit enlarges, and as it matures, its shape, colour, and texture also change. When a juicy, edible fruit such as this melon ripens, its flesh becomes very sweet and succulent.

The flower is brightly coloured and attracts insects that will pollinate it.

After pollination, the ovary starts to swell.

The flower is no longer needed, so it shrivels up and dies.

The fruit begins to form.

The fruit grows larger as it ripens.

The fruit has ripened and contains hundreds of seeds deep inside.

A melon is a kind of berry.

Parts of a seed

All seeds contain a tiny embryo and seed leaves called cotyledons, which are full of stored food. These are all enclosed in an outer seed coat, called a testa. The embryo has a minute root called a radicle and a tiny stem called a plumule. When the seed germinates, the food store provides nourishment for the tiny seedling.

Testa (seed coat)

Embryo

Cotyledon (seed leaf)

Testa

Apple seed

Cross-section of an apple seed

Seed dispersal

Plants need to spread their seeds to increase their chance of survival. Seeds are dispersed by wind, water, and animals. In some plants, parts of the fruit wall or flowerhead also help to spread the seeds. As the fruit dries, the fruit wall splits open and the seeds are scattered.

Dispersal by burial
Seeds are a valuable source of food for mammals and birds. Squirrels and other rodents bury acorns and other nuts, then forget to dig them up. These grow into plants where they were left.

Squirrel burying nuts

Bird dispersal
Brightly coloured orange and red berries attract birds, which like to feed on them. The birds swallow the berries whole but digest only the fleshy part. The seeds pass out, unharmed, in the bird's droppings.

Redwing

Water dispersal
Some fruits and seeds float. Their fruit wall contains oil droplets or air to make them buoyant. Coconut palm fruits float in the sea until they are washed up on a beach.

Coconut growing on a beach

Wind dispersal
Light fruits and seeds are spread by the wind. The seeds of a columbine are scattered when the breeze shakes the seed head. Maple tree seeds have papery wings to carry them on the wind.

Columbine seed head

Animal dispersal
Some seeds are encased inside hooked fruits that can easily become trapped in the fur of mammals. They are carried along by the animals and drop off later in another place.

Bison with seeds trapped in fur

Types of fruit

Simple fruits have a single ovary; compound fruits have more than one. When ripe, some fruits remain succulent; others become woody and hard, or dry and papery, such as larkspur. False fruits develop from other flower parts in addition to the ovary.

Berries
Berries have a combined mesocarp and endocarp layer. They often have many seeds that each have a tough seed coat, or testa.

Grapes

False fruits
In most false fruits, the receptacle swells to enclose the true fruit. Tiny true fruits may also be fixed to the surface of the receptacle.

Pear

Drupes
Drupes, or stone fruits, have a thick, fleshy mesocarp and a woody endocarp – the stone. Fruits such as raspberries are made up of many tiny drupelets.

Plum

Dry fruits
Dry fruits often have lids or seams that open to release the ripe seeds. This capsule has round openings called pores.

Love-in-a-mist capsule

FIND OUT MORE   BIRDS   FLOWERS   FOOD   MAMMALS   PLANTS   PLANTS, ANATOMY   PLANTS, REPRODUCTION   PLANT USES   RATS AND OTHER RODENTS

Succulent fruits

Berries

Kiwanos have a spiky rind to prevent animals from eating them until the seeds are ripe.

Avocados have a single large seed and oily flesh.

Redcurrant seeds are spread by birds.

Persimmons are juicy berries with many seeds.

Grapes each have a tiny stalk and grow in large clusters.

Tomato seeds are covered in a jelly layer that protects them while inside an animal's gut.

Melons are a firm-walled kind of berry called a pepo.

Gooseberry seeds are embedded in juicy flesh.

Lemons are citrus fruits with flesh made of juice-filled hairs.

Lychees have a fleshy layer that grows from the seed stalk.

Rambutans have very hairy skin.

Kiwis have black seeds embedded in firm green flesh.

Drupes and drupelets

Peaches have juicy flesh and a single seed protected inside a woody stone.

Cherries have a single seed inside a hard stone.

Apricots are cultivated fruits that have a single seed inside a woody stone.

Blackberry fruits each consist of many single-seeded drupelets.

Nectarines are a cultivated variety of peach with a smoother skin.

Damsons are small plums. Their seeds are spread when animals eat the flesh.

Mangoes have a large, single seed and sweet flesh.

Greengages are a kind of plum with green or yellow flesh.

Loganberries are made up of many single-seeded drupelets.

Plums have juicy flesh and a single seed inside a stone.

Sago palm fruits have a corky layer that allows them to float.

Coconuts are the fruit of a palm tree.

False fruits

Rowan berries are the swollen tips of the flower stem. They enclose the real fruit.

Apple flesh is the swollen tip of the flower stem, and the pips are the seeds.

Fig fruits are tiny woody pips contained in a fleshy swollen flower stem.

Strawberries consist of a red fleshy receptacle covered in tiny fruits.

Quinces have hard flesh and a seed-filled core.

Breadfruits have many fruits in a large, fleshy flowerhead.

Dry fruits

Honesty has a papery fruit and flat seeds.

Dandelion fruits have hairs that help them float in a breeze.

Goosegrass fruits have hooks that cling to animals' fur.

Sycamore fruits have wings that carry them on the wind.

Larkspur fruits split open to release the seeds.

Hogweed fruits are papery and contain two seeds.

Laburnum pods split to release the hard seeds.

Poppy capsules contain masses of tiny seeds.

Burdock has a head of hooked fruits.

Acorns are nuts with a tough, woody fruit wall.

Sweet chestnuts are enclosed in a spiny case.

Beech nuts are arranged in threes inside a rough case.

FURNITURE

EVERY DAY, PEOPLE SIT on chairs, sleep in beds, and eat from tables. All these are items of furniture, the movable equipment of a home. At one time, furniture was handmade, so most homes contained only basic, functional pieces. A wide range of more affordable furniture became available when production was mechanized in the 19th century. Today, furniture design is largely determined by function, cost, size, and fashion.

The chairs in this Roman sculpture are similar to modern chairs.

Antique furniture
Antiques are objects made more than 100 years ago. Antique furniture was usually handcrafted, using fine materials, in many different styles. Antiques are frequently considered valuable and are highly prized by collectors today.

Early furniture
Different cultures have produced very similar furniture. The ancient Egyptians had folding beds, and the Romans had armchairs. The earliest furniture to survive was sealed in Egyptian tombs.

An 18th-century cabinet

Types of furniture

Furniture made for use in a home is designed to be as comfortable as possible. Choices of shape and fabric let the buyer express personal taste. Office furniture is usually plainer and more functional. Furniture is found outdoors in the form of litter bins, street lamps, and bus stops.

Domestic furniture
Most homes have a bed or a futon. Originally created in Japan for modern, urban life, the futon saves space by serving as a bed at night and a sofa during the day.

Office furniture
Modern office furniture, such as this Anglepoise lamp, is designed to be practical, sturdy, and long-lasting.

The lamp head is easily adjusted.

The heavy base provides balance.

Street furniture
Despite having similar functions, street furniture looks very different all over the world. This elaborate public drinking fountain is in Paris, France.

How an armchair is made

Most modern furniture is mass-produced by machine rather than handcrafted. Furniture such as sofas and armchairs have machine-made parts that are fitted together by hand and then upholstered. This armchair is made from materials that have been built up around a wooden frame.

Steel springs attached to the frame help spread a person's weight evenly.

Arms are cushioned with foam padding and a fleece layer.

Upholsterer fits the fabric covering securely into position.

Castors are small wheels beneath the chair that allow it to be moved easily.

Metal springs make the chair comfortable to sit on.

Layers of metal mesh and hessian hold the springs in place.

Upholstery
A layer of padding called upholstery covers the basic wooden frame of a chair. Upholstery also refers to the way in which fabric is fitted to the frame. The top layer of fabric is chosen from a range of colours, patterns, and textures.

Cushions are filled with foam or feathers.

Fabric covering is durable.

Interior design
In furnishing a room, people try to choose colours, pictures, fabrics, and furniture that go well together. This process is known as interior design. It began in Europe in the 16th century, when furniture makers were first given charge of entire rooms to decorate as a unified whole.

Soft furnishings are materials such as rugs, cushions, and curtains. These materials are chosen to make a room comfortable and to help create its overall look.

Cushions and wallpaper borders are coordinated.

William Morris
The British designer, artist, and socialist William Morris (1834–96) was active in many areas. He was influential in the design of furniture and fabrics, argued for a return to handcrafted furniture, and founded the Arts and Crafts Movement for design.

FIND OUT MORE ARCHITECTURE   ART, HISTORY OF   CRAFTS   DESIGN   EGYPT, ANCIENT   HOUSES AND HOMES   MUSEUMS

English furniture

Lights

Iron candlestand,
late 17th century

Brass candlesticks,
early 18th century

Bronze storm lamp,
early 19th century

Gilt gaslight pendant,
mid 19th century

Glass electric pendant
with brass edgings, c.1900

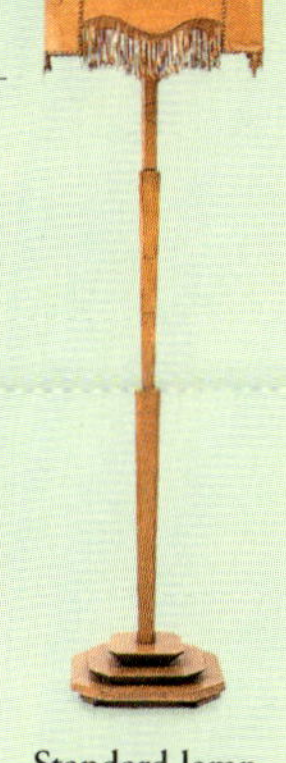

Standard lamp,
1930–40

Chairs

Carved oak armchair,
c.1620

Walnut chair,
c.1680

Beech armchair with
caned seat, c.1815

Upholstered chair with beech
and walnut frame, c.1860

**Ebonized beech
side-chair,** c.1890

**Birch veneered
plywood chair,** 1989

Tables and cabinets

Pine and oak side-table gilded
in Chinese style, c.1690

Mahogany and walnut table
on a tripod stand, c.1760

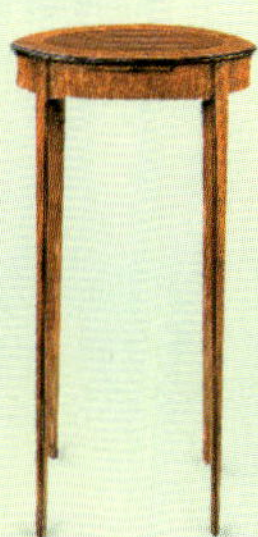

**Rosewood side-
table,** c.1800

**Combined games and
needlework table,** c.1830

Mahogany table in
Moorish style, c.1895

**Maple veneer side-
table,** late 1930s

Queen Anne cabinet on chest,
walnut veneer on a pine frame, c.1700

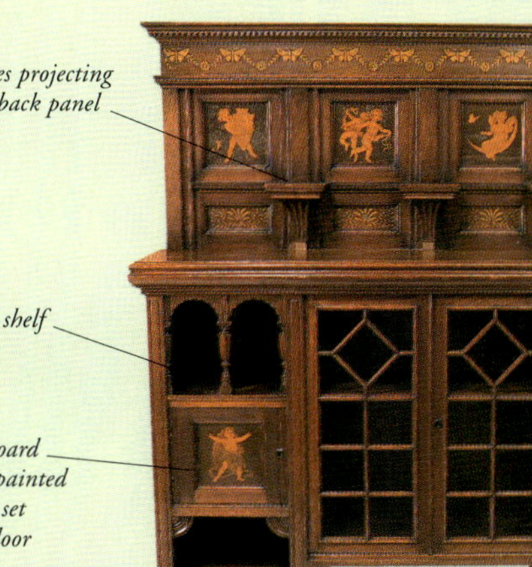

Mahogany cabinet with inset painted panels and
decoration, designed by Lewis F Day in 1880

Oak bookcase with fluted columns,
handcrafted in a traditional style, 1993

GALAXIES

A HUNDRED billion galaxies exist in the Universe. Each consists of a vast collection of stars, gas, and dust. They started life thousands of million of years ago, slowly forming into distinctive shapes. Each galaxy can contain billions of stars. Gravity keeps the stars together and keeps the galaxies in clusters.

Milky Way

About 500 billion stars make up the spiral-shaped Milky Way. The arms contain young, hot, bright stars; older, dimmer stars make up the nucleus. A thin halo of old stars surrounds our Galaxy. The Sun is in one of the arms, about two-thirds of the way from the centre. It orbits the centre of the Galaxy once every 220 million years.

The Milky Way is about 100,000 light years wide and 13,000 light years across at the central hub.

Types of galaxies

Most galaxies have a central ball of stars, the nucleus, and many have a flattened disc coming out of this. Astronomers have classified galaxies into three main types based on these features. No one knows why galaxies become a particular shape. It may be to do with how fast a galaxy spins and how quickly stars form inside.

Elliptical

About 60 per cent of galaxies are ball-shaped collections of old stars. They range in shape from round to flattened ovals. Astronomers describe their shape with the letter *E* followed by a number between *0* and *7* – the higher the number, the flatter the galaxy.

Spiral

A hub of older stars is surrounded by a flattened disc with spiral arms containing younger stars. The shape of a spiral is described by the letter *S*, followed by a letter between *a* and *d* to indicate how tightly wound the arms are and the size of the hub.

Irregular

About 10 per cent of galaxies are irregular. They are collections of stars with no distinctive shape or structure, and do not fit into any of the classifications. They are smaller than the average galaxy and contain large amounts of gas and dust.

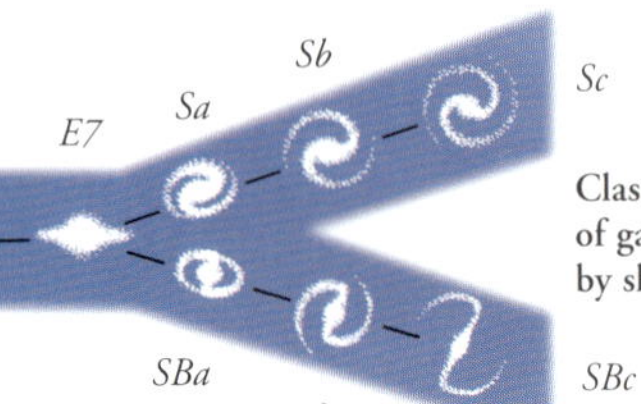

Barred spiral

These galaxies consist of a central bar of older stars with arms containing younger stars coming from the ends of the bar. Barred spirals are described as *SB* followed by a letter from *a* to *d* to indicate how tightly wound the arms are and the size of the hub.

Active galaxies

Unusually large amounts of energy are emitted from some galaxies. This energy may come from an object that is visible, such as a quasar, or from an invisible object, such as the lobes of a radio galaxy. How the energy is created is uncertain, but evidence suggests it could be from a supermassive black hole at the centre of the galaxy.

Quasars

Quasars are the brightest, most distant, fastest moving, and youngest objects visible outside the Milky Way. Thousands are known, each emitting huge amounts of energy. They are found at the heart of large galaxies.

Radio galaxies

Powerful radio energy is emitted by radio galaxies. The energy comes from lobes at either side of the visible core, and is detectable with radio telescopes. Centaurus A is the nearest active galaxy: it is 16 million light years away.

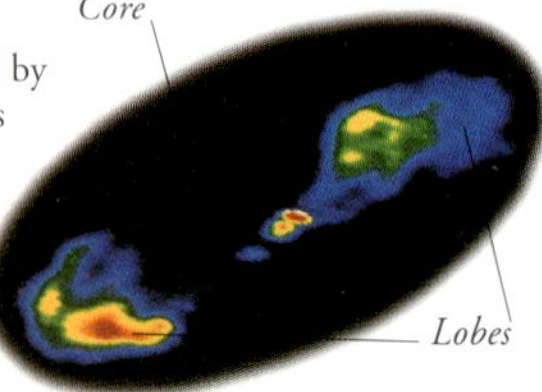

Centaurus A

Colliding galaxies

Galaxies can collide as they move through space, as is happening (left) with two galaxies in the constellation of Boötes. Such collisions will change the shape of a galaxy or result in a merger.

Edwin Hubble

In 1923, the American astronomer Edwin Hubble (1889–1953) proved that there are galaxies other than the Milky Way. The next year he classified galaxies according to their shape. He went on to show that galaxies are moving away from each other, and so provided proof that the Universe is expanding.

Galaxy clusters

Galaxies are grouped together in clusters. The Milky Way belongs to a cluster of about 30 galaxies called the Local Group. The Virgo Cluster (right) contains about 2,500 galaxies, mostly spirals.

Superclusters

Clusters of galaxies group together into superclusters that spread across many millions of light years. In turn, hundreds of superclusters group together to form huge walls and filaments, such as the Stick Man, which stretch for hundreds of millions of light years.

The Stick Man contains millions of galaxies.

FIND OUT MORE   ASTRONOMY   BIG BANG   BLACK HOLES   GRAVITY   STARS   UNIVERSE

GALILEO GALILEI

THE ITALIAN SCIENTIST Galileo Galilei was one of the greatest astronomers and physicists of all time. He was the first person to use a telescope to look at the heavens. He started a branch of physics called mechanics, showing that nature obeyed mathematical rules. His belief that science should be based on observation made him one of the first modern scientists. It also led him into trouble, because his views about the Solar System went against those held by the Roman Catholic Church.

Early life
Galileo was born in Pisa, Italy, in 1564. After school he went to the University of Pisa to study medicine. But Galileo was more interested in mathematics and physics, and left without a degree. By the time he was 25, he was back at the university – as professor of mathematics.

Telescope
In 1609, Galileo heard of the invention of the telescope and made one of his own. He used it to look at the heavens and made many astronomical discoveries. He noticed that the planet Venus has phases like the Moon. This gave support to the theory of Nicolaus Copernicus that the planets went round the Sun.

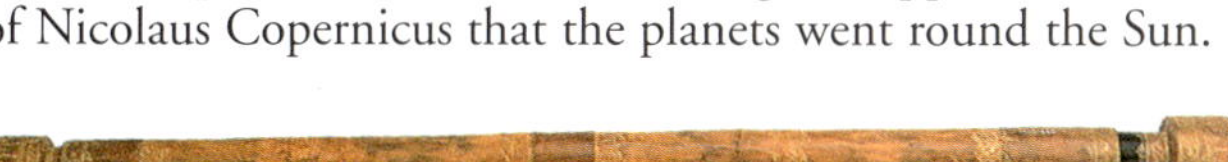
Replica of Galileo's telescope, 1609

Moving bodies
In the 16th century, people believed that the Sun moved around Earth. Galileo did not agree with this, and developed Copernicus's theory of Earth moving around the Sun.

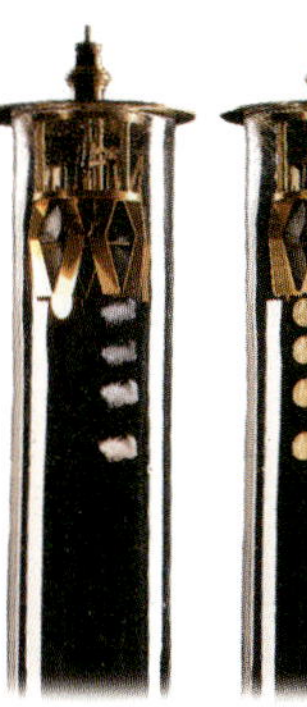
Falling feather

Coin falls at same speed

Gravity
Galileo showed that all objects fall at the same speed, no matter what their weight. Previously, people had believed that heavier objects fell faster. There is a story that Galileo proved his theory by dropping objects from the leaning tower of Pisa, but this is probably not true. He certainly did an experiment like this, in which objects of different weights were dropped in identical jars from which the air was pumped out.

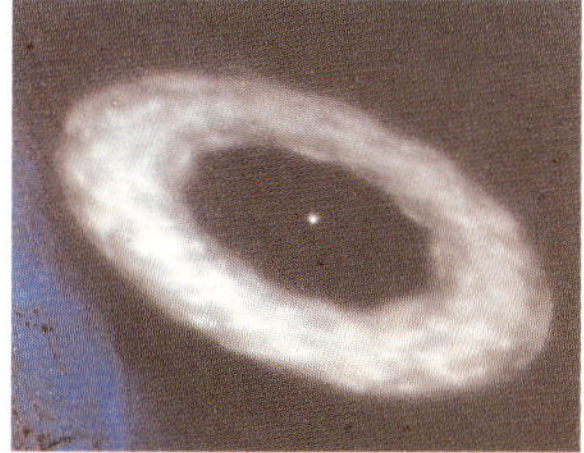
Artist's impression of the Milky Way

Milky Way
In 1610, Galileo built a telescope that could magnify 1,000 times. It enabled him to see thousands of stars that no human being had ever seen before. He trained his new telescope on the Milky Way and found that it was a vast collection of stars, clustered together in groups of various sizes.

Planet with two moons

Planet with ringlike formations

Galileo's drawings of Saturn

Planets and moons
Through his telescope, Galileo saw what he at first thought were two small moons orbiting the planet Saturn. He drew these "moons" in his notebooks, but later worked out that they were Saturn's now-famous rings. He also discovered the four moons that orbit the planet Jupiter, and was able to examine the craters on our own Moon.

The Starry Messenger
In March 1610, Galileo published many of his discoveries in his book, *The Starry Messenger*. The book also showed that Copernicus was right to say that the Earth moved around the Sun, and that the Roman Catholic Church's idea of an unmoving Earth at the centre of the Universe was wrong. *The Starry Messenger* infuriated many churchmen.

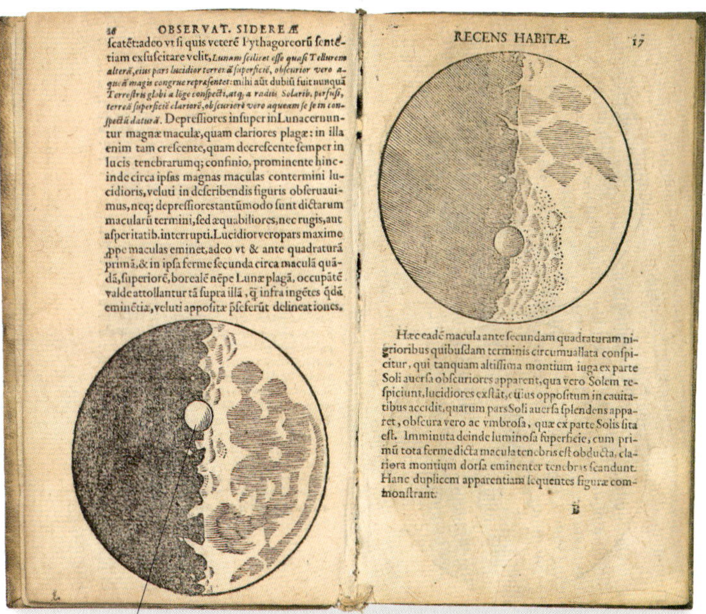
Crater on Moon

Illustrated pages from *The Starry Messenger*, 1610

Inquisition
Galileo's support for Copernicus's ideas outraged the Catholic Church because the priests thought that the Earth should be at the centre of the Universe. In 1633, the Church called Galileo to appear before its court, or inquisition, in Rome. The court ordered him to deny his beliefs under threat of torture. Galileo was forced to agree that Earth was the centre of the Universe, but was heard to mutter, "Yet it *does* move".

Trial of Galileo

FIND OUT MORE

FORCE AND MOTION · PLANETS · SCIENCE, HISTORY OF · STARS · SUN AND SOLAR SYSTEM · TELESCOPES

GANDHI, MOHANDAS

WHEN THE VAST AND HEAVILY populated nation of India gained independence from Britain in August 1947, one man more than any other was responsible for that achievement. Mohandas Gandhi united the different communities of India and led them to independence. He believed in non-violent protest and despised the racial violence of his homeland. He became known as Mahatma, or "great soul". Although he did not live long enough to see the results of his work, Gandhi is remembered today as the instigator of three movements crucial in the 20th century: the campaigns against racism, colonialism, and violence.

Early life

Mohandas Kamarchand Gandhi was born in Porbandar, India, in 1869. Educated in India and Britain, he trained in law and became a barrister in 1889. In 1893 he moved to work in South Africa. While there, he edited a newspaper called *Indian Opinion* and campaigned against racial injustice, forcing the South African government to grant Indians rights of permanent citizenship in 1914.

Indian nationalism

The British had controlled India since the 18th century, but many Indians wanted to govern themselves. In 1915, Gandhi returned from South Africa and became one of the leaders of the independence movement. He led many peaceful campaigns against British rule, using the tactic of non-violent civil disobedience. He called this method Satyagraha ("holding to the truth"). It was copied by many civil-rights campaigners around the world.

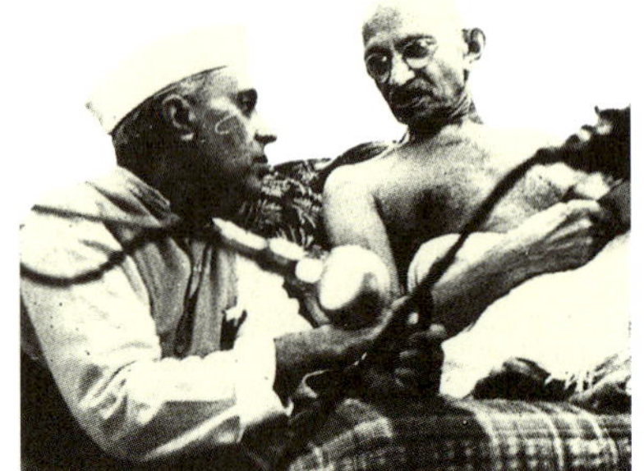

Gandhi with Jawaharlal Nehru, leader of the socialist wing of Congress

Congress

The Indian National Congress Party was founded in 1885. Its members wanted to increase Indian participation in government and represent all religions and cultures. During the 1920s, under the leadership of Gandhi and Jawaharlal Nehru, Congress took the lead in campaigning for Indian independence.

Imprisonment

During his many campaigns, Gandhi was often imprisoned by the British for civil disobedience. But after each spell in prison, Gandhi emerged more powerful and more respected than before. His personal prestige was so high that people began to call him Mahatma, the "great soul". He alone seemed able to unite the diverse elements of the independence movement that represented the many different religions and cultures in the huge subcontinent of India.

Gandhi's sandals

Gandhi's spectacles

Gandhi lived a simple life, wearing plain clothes and keeping only a few possessions.

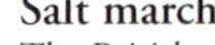

Gandhi's watch

Salt march

The British controlled the production of salt in India. This monopoly forced up prices and was very unpopular. In 1930, Gandhi led a 320-km (200-mile) march to the sea to get his own salt and thousands joined him on the way. Gandhi was imprisoned for civil disobedience, but the march showed the power of Satyagraha.

Social reforms

In 1937, the Indian provinces received a large measure of home rule. The Congress Party took control of seven of the 11 provinces and began to reform the country. Gandhi pushed for social, economic, and educational improvements designed to rebuild India. He encouraged crafts such as spinning cotton, because he believed that small cottage industries could help India's villages.

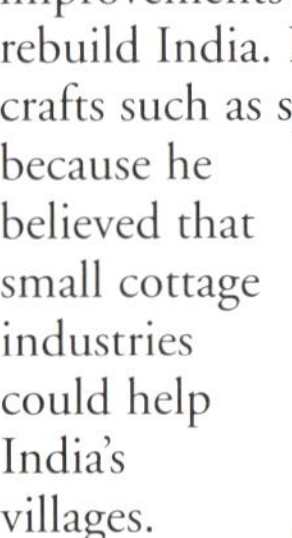

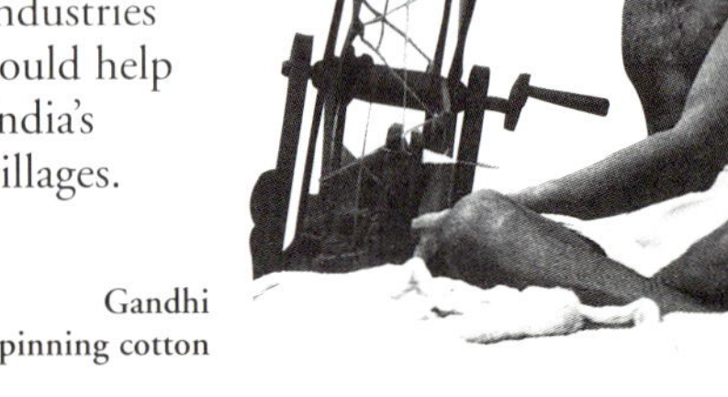

Gandhi spinning cotton

Independence

In 1947, India gained its independence. Hindus in the Congress Party wanted a united India, but Muslims wanted a country of their own. The country was, therefore, divided into India and Pakistan, a division Gandhi bitterly opposed.

Assassination

Gandhi took little part in the independence talks, but threatened to fast to death to protest against the violence between Hindus and Muslims. In January 1948, he was assassinated by a Hindu fanatic who resented his concern for the Muslims.

Monument at the place where Gandhi died

MOHANDAS GANDHI

1869	Born in Porbandar, India.
1889	Becomes a barrister in England.
1891–93	Works as a lawyer in India.
1893–1915	Works in South Africa.
1920s	Takes control of Congress Party with Nehru.
1930	Leads salt march to the sea.
1942	Launches Quit India campaign during World War II, and is interned until 1944.
1945	New British government promises independence by 1947.
1947	India gains its independence.
1948	Gandhi is assassinated.

FIND OUT MORE   EMPIRES   HINDUISM   HUMAN RIGHTS   INDIA, HISTORY OF   SOUTH AFRICA, HISTORY OF

GARBO, GRETA

SOPHISTICATED, SUPERIOR, scornful, and beautiful, Greta Garbo was everyone's idea of the perfect film star. The daughter of a poor labourer in Stockholm, Sweden, she conquered Hollywood in the 1920s and 1930s. Her audiences adored her, but at the height of her career she retired, becoming a recluse and never showing her face in public again. Yet this most celebrated actor received no Oscars, only a belated special award for her unforgettable films.

Early life

Greta Gustafson was born in the Swedish capital of Stockholm in 1905. Her family was poor, and she worked from an early age in a barber's shop and a department store. Her first film part was in *How Not to Dress*, a publicity film for the store.

Training

Early in her career, Garbo appeared as the female lead in a slapstick comedy, *Peter the Tramp*. She then applied for and won a scholarship to Sweden's Royal Dramatic Theatre training school, where she was soon playing small parts on stage.

Mauritz Stiller

While at training school, Garbo was spotted by the Swedish film director Mauritz Stiller. Stiller was best known for such films as the comedy *Love and Journalism*, and the sexually charged movie *Erotikon*. Stiller took a special interest in Garbo's career, gave her the surname Garbo, and made her into a star.

Garbo and Mauritz Stiller

First success

Garbo's first major film role was as the star of *The Atonement of Gösta Berling*. The film was a romantic tale of a priest set in the Swedish countryside. The premiere in Stockholm in 1924 attracted a huge audience and launched Garbo on her film career.

Still from *Gösta Berling*

Hollywood

In 1925, after the success of *Gösta Berling,* Garbo moved to Hollywood, the centre of the US film industry. She signed a contract with Metro-Goldwyn-Mayer (MGM) and began filming *The Torrent*. Her first major success was *Flesh and the Devil*, made in 1926 and directed by Clarence Brown. By 1927, she was earning $5,000 a week from MGM. In all, Garbo made 24 films in Hollywood, and became one of the most famous, and best-paid, film stars in the world.

A life apart

In 1941, Garbo announced her retirement from making films, having no wish to disappoint her admirers by growing old on screen. Despite her success in Europe, her popularity was declining in the USA. She became an American citizen in 1951 and led the life of a recluse, although she remained friends with many famous people.

"I want to be alone" was Garbo's famous wish after her retirement in 1941.

"Garbo talks!"

In 1930, the first sound film starring Garbo appeared. The publicity slogan was "Garbo talks!". The film, *Anna Christie,* had a heroine with a Swedish accent. The producers thought this would be an ideal role for Garbo. They believed that audiences might not otherwise accept her heavily accented voice.

Studio system

Film-making in Hollywood was dominated by a few large companies, such as MGM, Paramount, and Warner Bros. These and other studios kept actors and directors on tight contracts, so that they could not work for a rival company. As a result, Garbo was forced to star in films she did not like.

Anna Karenina

Garbo's reputation as a tragic heroine was established by *Anna Karenina* (1935), based on the novel by the great Russian writer Leo Tolstoy. The film won numerous awards and confirmed Garbo's reputation as the leading actress of her day.

Garbo laughs

Garbo's reputation was as a serious, intense actress. In 1939, she astounded audiences with her relaxed performance in the romantic comedy *Ninotchka.* Publicity for the film made much of her laughter in this role.

FIND OUT MORE

CAMERAS   FILMS AND FILM-MAKING   LITERATURE

GARDENS

LIKE LANDSCAPES in miniature, gardens are set-aside areas of land where plants are grown to provide beauty and relaxation. Gardens have a practical purpose too. From ancient times, they have helped people nurture plants for food and medicine. They reduce noise and air pollution in cities, and create a refreshing environment in a hot climate. Glorious landscaped gardens can enhance the finest modern buildings, and botanic gardens are places of scientific study.

Tools

Gardeners use a variety of tools. Some have hardly changed in hundreds of years, such as forks. Mechanical aids such as the lawnmower, invented in 1832, are relatively new developments.

Shears, for cutting hedges

Thick blades

Used for digging soil

Spade and fork

Watering can

Trowel

Hand fork

Development of gardens

Gardens have an ancient history. They were planted in Mesopotamia, China, Egypt, Persia, and Greece. The Romans spread knowledge of gardening to northern Europe during their rule of the Mediterranean lands. From the 4th century AD, when Roman power declined, monks continued the tradition of cultivating plants in monastery gardens. European gardens were enclosed by abbey or castle walls until the Renaissance.

China and Japan

Gardens in China and Japan often have a religious significance, where nature itself is honoured. This tradition is centuries old. For Zen Buddhists, landscaped gardens of raked gravel, where a rock may represent a mountain, are places of silent meditation.

Gravel, raked into patterns

Clipped shrubs

Temple garden, Kyoto, Japan

Islamic gardens

North African Moors created shady courtyard gardens, with pools and fountains to reflect the sky and cool the air. When they conquered Spain in the 8th century, the Moors took the style to Europe, as seen in the Court of the Myrtles, the Alhambra, Spain.

Renaissance formality

During the Renaissance in the 14th century, architects planned gardens as settings for the grand houses they designed. Fashionable gardens were formal, open, and regular, reviving a style established by the Romans.

Villa Lante, Bagnaia, Lazio, Italy

Botanic gardens

In botanic gardens, specimen plants are collected and cultivated for scientific study. They developed from the herb or physic gardens tended by medieval monks, where plants were grown for medicinal purposes.

18th-century naturalism

The Jardin Anglais (English garden) style spread through Europe during the 18th century. The trend was first set by the English architect William Kent (c.1685–1748), who planned less formal gardens than had been common previously. He used an open style, which he believed to look more natural, to set off the formality of his buildings.

This small Classical temple, in a wooded glade, is typical of the Jardin Anglais style.

Chiswick House, London, England

Plant collectors

From the late 1600s, European explorers returned from their world expeditions with many new and exotic varieties of plant. Serious plant-collecting expeditions began in the 18th century, bringing back specimens for scientific study and to decorate gardens.

The peony, a native of China, was taken to Europe by plant collectors.

Roberto Burle Marx

Brazilian garden designer Roberto Burle Marx (1909–1994) created stunning gardens for modern buildings in Brazil, using only plants native to his country. He made Brazilians more aware of the amazing plants found in their countryside.

Wildlife gardens

In the 20th century, gardeners became more interested in the wild creatures that inhabited their plants, trees, and ponds. Instead of treating them as pests, they welcomed wildlife. Careful planting of a wildlife garden creates many different habitats, encouraging the widest possible range of animal visitors.

Gardeners plant flowers that attract insects.